COLIN CRAWFORD was born in Belfast in 1948 and [...]
and the Royal Belfast Academical Institution. Hav[...]
social work training in Croydon in 1974, he was a prison welfare officer in Long
Kesh until 1979, when he resigned following the leaking of his M.Sc. degree
research, which established that the government's criminalisation policy was
likely to lead to a serious escalation of the conflict in Northern Ireland. In 1995
he was nominated as a spokesperson by loyalist prisoners and former prisoners
'to articulate their views and perspectives' at the Forum for Peace and
Reconciliation in Dublin. Holding higher degrees from Queen's University
Belfast, the Cranfield Institute and the University of Bradford, he currently
lectures in Applied Social Studies at the University of Ulster.

DEFENDERS OR CRIMINALS?

Loyalist prisoners and criminalisation

COLIN CRAWFORD

THE
BLACKSTAFF
PRESS
—
BELFAST

First published in 1999 by
The Blackstaff Press Limited
Blackstaff House, Wildflower Way, Apollo Road, Belfast BT12 6TA, Northern Ireland

This book has received support from the
Cultural Diversity Programme of the Community Relations Council,
which aims to encourage acceptance and understanding of cultural diversity.
The views expressed do not necessarily reflect those of the
NI Community Relations Council.

Typeset by Techniset Typesetters, Newton-le-Willows, Merseyside

Printed in England by Biddles Limited

A CIP catalogue record for this book
is available from the British Library

ISBN 0-85640-649-X

for
Henry James (Harry) Crawford

Contents

Preface

I joined the Northern Ireland Probation Service in 1971 and was subsequently seconded for professional social work training at Croydon College, south-east London (1972–4). Upon completion of training I was appointed as a prison welfare officer and dispatched to Long Kesh. From 1974 I worked with Special Category prisoners, ordinary criminal offenders and young offenders. By 1975 I was undertaking research through the Cranfield Institute, examining the advantages of the Special Category compound system of imprisonment, and comparing it with conventional criminal systems. This research demonstrated that Special Category prisoners were quite different from their criminal counterparts, both in terms of motivation and background, and that the compound system was a humane containment model of imprisonment, which avoided the institutional oppression and alienation commonly found in criminal systems.

In 1976 the British government introduced its criminalisation policy, whereby Special Category status was phased out, and subsequently prisoners who would have been eligible for such status were 'criminalised'. As they were to become the new criminal prisoner population, existing criminal offenders became officially described as 'ordinary decent criminals', or ODCs, to differentiate the two populations.

By 1979 I had completed my research which highlighted the advantages of Special Category status, not only upon criminological criteria but, much more importantly, as part of a conflict resolution strategy. The research also pointed to the dangers of the government's criminalisation policy leading to an escalation of the conflict. The findings were 'leaked' to the media, and I resigned.

For some years afterwards I retained a research association with loyalist prisoners, forming particular relationships which were to prove significant.

In 1995, after perhaps a decade of virtually no contact with loyalist prisoners or their organisations, I received a telephone call from Tim O'Connor, of the Forum for Peace and Reconciliation secretariat in Dublin. I was told that I had been nominated by 'loyalists' to represent and 'articulate the views and perspectives of loyalist prisoners and former prisoners' at the forum. I was accordingly appointed to the Dublin forum as a 'Special Category' observer in April 1995.

This book grew out of my re-established contact with loyalist paramilitary groups and loyalist prisoners.

COLIN CRAWFORD
UNIVERSITY OF ULSTER AT JORDANSTOWN
FEBRUARY 1999

Acknowledgements

Research and writing can be lonely activities which often take place against competing demands upon time. In this research I was very fortunate to have had the unwavering support and encouragement of John White of the Ulster Democratic Party.

Anonymity was crucial in this research with paramilitary ex-prisoners, and an assurance of absolute confidentiality was a necessary prerequisite to almost all of the interviews. Accordingly, I cannot name those people I should like to thank, particularly as many of them feel that there may be a return to open conflict in Northern Ireland. However, I am most grateful to them all and I sincerely thank them.

I should also like to extend my thanks to the staff and volunteers of the Ex-Prisoners' Interpretative Centre and the Prisoners' Aid and Post-Conflict Resettlement Group. Both these organisations generously gave of their time in making the crucial contacts with most of the former prisoners interviewed. My thanks also to Gusty Spence and other members of the Progressive Unionist Party, and the Ulster Democratic Party, for their advice and support.

Many thanks to the staff of Blackstaff Press whose support, commitment and professionalism was invaluable.

My thanks to Ruth Tovey for having the courage and patience to undertake the typing of yet another scribbled manuscript, when I could not look at it again.

And finally, thanks to my wife Gillian for her understanding and encouragement during a protracted period of writing and research.

PART ONE

Introduction

A vast amount of literature has been amassed tracing the history and evolution of the republican movement and, in particular, the Irish Republican Army (IRA). Much of this work is excellent, and some of it is deeply sympathetic in its portrayal of republicanism, presenting its objectives as rational and comprehensible. There is little comparable analysis of loyalism or of the militant loyalists' cause, and where it does exist it tends to be unsympathetic and profoundly critical. Notably, the case of loyalist political prisoners has been neglected.

Some writers contend that there may exist a deliberate stifling of literature on loyalism. Others, some loyalists among them, maintain that academic enquiry into loyalism and loyalist paramilitaries has not been of a quality to merit publication (with a few notable exceptions). Whatever the truth, there is a striking imbalance in the literature on these two paramilitary cultures.

Militant loyalism, in common with militant republicanism, has been guilty of horrific acts against humanity. This is the unpalatable reality of war or civil conflict. The conflict in Northern Ireland was not acted out by mercenary armies but by ordinary people who 'became involved' or 'went active'. Like republicans, loyalists who joined the Protestant paramilitaries were politically motivated, acting, as they saw it, in defence of their country.

In Northern Ireland some loyalist and unionist communities bore almost the full brunt of republican terrorism. They watched as their cities, towns and villages were devastated in bomb blasts, and they watched as their fellow countrymen and women – civilians, children, police officers and soldiers – were maimed, injured and killed in bombings and shootings. They stood by as their institutions of defence, including the B Specials, were shamed and disbanded, and they observed as the British security forces, lacking in will or capability, proved to be almost ineffectual in combating the increasingly strident republican war machine. And then they began to detect a growing British weariness with Northern Ireland and feared most of all that a British withdrawal was becoming high on the government's agenda.

With a sense of abandonment and betrayal in the face of escalating republican violence, loyalists engaged the IRA, and the nationalist community, with the same tactics of war as had been visited upon them. By 1972 loyalist paramilitaries were a risen force whose campaign would eventually match and even exceed republican terrorism in a war which was essentially to involve the politics of fear. This book will attempt to make a contribution to the analysis of that history from the perspective of those loyalists who were part of it.

1

The Emergence of the
Loyalist Paramilitary Organisations

Many loyalists take the view that their paramilitary campaign was a reactive one, waged in response to republican violence. It is true that the Ulster Volunteer Force (UVF) re-emerged in the 1960s, but its emergence was essentially symbolic. During this period it carried a potential rather than an actual serious paramilitary capability. In June 1966 the UVF was responsible for the killing of two Catholic men in Belfast in separate incidents. The ensuing arrest and imprisonment of three UVF men, including Gusty Spence, virtually closed down all UVF operations at that time. Subsequently there was little evidence of any residual military structure and, as Steve Bruce comments, 'surprisingly little organised support'.[1]

Had the UVF been a more organised and competent paramilitary force in the late sixties and early seventies it would have been well placed to provide and co-ordinate leadership for the emerging loyalist vigilante groups. As it was, under almost farcical circumstances, an Ulster Defence Association (UDA) leadership emerged from within the vigilantes, a leadership that was unsophisticated, strategically inept and totally outclassed by the Provisional IRA.

Belfast had been no stranger to sectarian conflict, but the scale and nature of the new IRA offensive during 1970 to 1971 was without precedent in Northern Ireland. By the end of 1970, 23 civilians and 2 police officers had been killed, and there had been 153 explosions across the country. Republican violence was stepped up in 1971, its outrages including the murder of three Scottish soldiers, lured to their deaths by female IRA operatives in March, and the bombing of the Mountainview

Tavern on the loyalist Shankill Road in May, when many customers were seriously injured. Protests, street battles, house burnings and intimidation followed the introduction of internment in August, forcing hundreds of Belfast families to flee their homes.

By September 1971 the UDA had an estimated membership of 40,000 – 50,000, representing the full spectrum of working-class loyalism. In the full knowledge that the loyalists had mobilised an army, the Provisionals embarked upon a series of highly provocative attacks, including another bombing on the Shankill, this time at the Four Step Inn, which killed two people and injured twenty. In December the UVF retaliated by bombing McGurk's bar in the nationalist New Lodge in north Belfast, killing fifteen people and injuring eight. This was the first serious loyalist bomb attack. By the end of the year there had been over one thousand bomb explosions, the vast majority carried out by the Provisionals; the republicans had killed 111 people, the loyalists 23.

Not only was the loyalists' military capability much weaker than the republicans', their handling of the media was openly hostile. On the back of the civil rights campaign, republicans groomed and courted the press to their advantage. Loyalists, on the other hand, clearly lacking in any public relations skills, physically threatened the journalists who crowded into Northern Ireland intent on reporting the Troubles to an international audience. Their behaviour carried what should have been fairly obvious implications for their subsequent portrayal worldwide, a portrayal so negative it prompted loyalists to behave in an even more hostile manner, in a round of encounters which rapidly became a vicious circle.

There were, of course, competent, high-calibre loyalist volunteers, but they found themselves without effective leadership. Officers, traditionally drawn from the middle classes and upon whom the rank and file depended, had failed to come forward, leaving the organisation weak in the strategic planning that was so desperately needed. Ordinary working-class men, without the relevant training or education, fell into positions of power disproportionate to their ability. By and large these were unemployed men who could devote time to their new roles, and who often spent a considerable amount of their time in bars and drinking clubs. The result was inevitable – in the early stages of the conflict, and later, the loyalist response to the IRA tended to be more instinctual than intellectual, emotional as opposed to rational, and spontaneous rather than strategic. This contrasted with a highly organised, well-trained and tactically minded republican force, which successfully carried out its terrorist campaign and confidently articulated its cause.

Another significant contrast between militant loyalists and republicans lay within differences of culture and tradition. Like the original UVF, formed in 1912 to fight Irish home rule, militant loyalists depended upon direction from the unionist establishment. Militant republicans, however, found direction and inspiration from an enduring political philosophy, a broadly based grass-roots support, and one overriding objective – Irish unification. In short, at the start of the Troubles the IRA had standing orders, operational strategy and a coherent *raison d'être*, which could be traced back to the Easter Rising of 1916 and even earlier. On the other hand, traumatised and insecure, the UVF and the emerging UDA were deeply divided over opposing political objectives – the full integration of Northern Ireland into the United Kingdom, or the establishment of a negotiated independent state.

Some nationalists spoke of the 'myth of the Protestant backlash' as loyalist paramilitaries slowly and falteringly organised. There were few willing to risk arrest and imprisonment, injury and death, advancing a militant loyalist agenda, but in the end the increasing stridency of republican violence served as an effective catalyst. By 1971 many of the new loyalist volunteers were frustrated that no loyalist grouping was sufficiently organised, or sufficiently militant, to respond to what they perceived to be IRA attacks on the Protestant state and the Union. Added to this frustration was a sense of isolation – loyalists felt deeply let down both by the Loyal Orders and by unionist politicians, who had failed to protect and support them. Also, the British Army, in which so many loyalists had served, not only failed to take their side but on occasion acted against them. And finally, they found there was no fellow-feeling for, or identification with, their cause in London that, in any way, matched the support in the South readily give to republicans.

While all these factors combined to deepen loyalist anxiety, it was the apparent lack of political commitment in Westminster towards maintaining the Union that was felt to be most fundamentally threatening. As J. Bowyer Bell comments:

> Generally both Labour and the Tories wanted most of all an end to the 'Irish intrusion', law and order, peace and quiet, at worst an acceptable level of violence with a continuing military presence with the odd

atrocity; at best they wanted an accommodation that would cork the bottle. The Anglo-Irish Treaty of 1921 had corked that bottle once, corked it for fifty years, and what was needed, nearly everyone in London felt, was another such accommodation; the return of Lloyd George, not more Black and Tans. London always sought conciliation, institutionalised compromise, to end a crisis, but only when that crisis escalated . . . the British establishment looked for an out.[2]

The loyalists, however, were not going to provide the British with an 'out'. For them the equation was enduringly simple – it was Union, or war. The Provisionals had all to win; the loyalists had all to lose. A *Loyalist News* statement in August 1971 accurately captures the loyalist mood at the time:

> The Protestant way of life was under open siege. The Loyal institutions . . . had not responded. The appropriate response was paramilitary, extraconstitutional, local and defensive. This was the fundamental response, traditional, only novel in that trustworthy leadership seemed to be lacking. So the people of God must act for themselves.[3]

The British had indirectly, and directly, presided over a corrupt and discriminatory state from its inception in 1922 until the outbreak of the conflict in 1969. The sectarian nature of the Northern Ireland state has been well documented. Characterised by discrimination and oppression, unionist and Protestant ascendancy, it institutionalised Catholic disadvantage. There is no doubt that this was fuelled by unionist self-interest, but it was also motivated by a fear of the republican enemy within. Not surprisingly, such a sustained period of oppression had the inevitable political consequence. However, when the civil rights activists took to the streets in 1968, loyalists genuinely did not understand the nature and basis of the protests and marches. Working-class Protestants felt that they had suffered the same deprivations and disadvantages as working-class Catholics. On top of that there was an endemic cultural resistance to understanding legitimate Catholic grievance. Instead, loyalists believed what they had always been taught to believe – that any protest by Catholics was insurrection, behind which lay the gunmen of the IRA. A view, which as events unfolded, they felt justified in holding.

Secret London talks in July 1972 between British government ministers and the Provisional IRA's high command did not serve the cause of loyalism or help to bolster loyalist paramilitary confidence. Rather, it was viewed as evidence of a British betrayal. Earlier that year the

Provisionals had greeted as a victory the prorogation of the Stormont parliament and the introduction of direct rule from Westminster. The loyalists only saw the punitive loss of their own local parliament under IRA pressure. It was in these circumstances that the 'mass movement' loyalist paramilitaries, including the UDA and the UFF, were formed. The UVF had asserted its paramilitary capability with the bombing of McGurk's bar and other incidents. By the summer of 1972, in response to pressures and demands from within its own community for defence and protection, it eventually came together as a cohesive force. The loyalist paramilitaries felt that they had understood what the British and the unionists had failed to grasp – the country was facing a sophisticated and ruthless republican war machine and consequently a campaign of counter-terrorism could no longer be avoided.

The UVF had within its ranks volunteers who, as former British soldiers in Cyprus, Borneo and Malaya, knew only too well the limitations of conventional forces in combating terrorism. They had been involved in carrying out covert counter-terrorist measures, including 'dirty tricks', as they were known. Perhaps more significantly, some UVF volunteers were intimately acquainted with Anglo-Irish history of 1916–21. Many of the older men had joined with the first wave of UVF recruits in 1912, and others, as members of the Royal Irish Constabulary (RIC) and the Black and Tans, had seen action in the Anglo-Irish War. They passed their wisdom and their distrust of British intention on to the younger generation. Some had witnessed first hand the British defeat in Ireland and were well aware of the British capacity for strategic and tactical blunders. They were also aware of British desire to put an end to the 'Irish problem', and they knew that an augmented British presence in Northern Ireland could, paradoxically, increase the threat to the Northern Ireland state. They fully understood, as did the IRA, that an 'oppressive' British Army presence would heighten nationalist and republican alienation, which in turn would be converted into support for a republican armed struggle.

The British Army was also the greatest obstacle to the loyalists engaging the IRA. As Gusty Spence explained in the early 1970s:

> Often we have fought the IRA at long range. I'd like to get a wee bit closer. Unfortunately we can't. To get to these IRA people, you have to go through British lines. As 80% of our members are ex-servicemen,

they would never dream of firing on a British soldier. The British are, to a large degree, holding us back.[4]

Loyalist literature stated the case even more starkly: 'To win the civil war what do we need? The first inevitable point is the removal of the British army.'[5]

The loyalist paramilitaries duly embarked upon the brutal and ruthless 'dirty war' tactics required in a counter-terrorist campaign. Some loyalist strategists reasoned that the IRA had to be made aware that if loyalists, or the wider Protestant community, suffered from republican terrorism, then the republican and nationalist communities would bear the brunt of equally harsh counter-terrorism. (Some loyalists contend that there was no coincidence in the announcement of the IRA cease-fire in 1994 and loyalist counter-terrorist measures exceeding republican terrorism.)

Isolated and ostracised by their own political leaders, the loyalist paramilitaries duly waged their campaign, largely reactively, against the IRA and republicanism from 1972 until the Combined Loyalist Military Command (CLMC) cease-fire in 1994. During that time they were to develop very considerably not only in terms of their military and strategic capability but also in political awareness. Since the early days of loyalist militarism, the loyalist paramilitaries have undergone an impressive political metamorphosis. While undoubtedly retaining a capacity for war, their politicisation has reached a stage where they are more willing than the mainstream unionists to seek compromise and accommodation with the Catholic community. The leaders of the loyalist fringe parties, the Ulster Democratic Party (UDP), representing the UDA and the UFF, and the Progressive Unionist Party (PUP), representing the UVF, have no difficulty with the principle of 'parity of esteem' for all citizens in Northern Ireland, or with a Bill of Rights which would actively promote non-discriminatory policies.

The significance of this shift in attitude – from one of tribal sectarianism to a willingness for political accommodation – cannot be overstated. It bears testament to the fact that real change has been achieved in Northern Ireland, a change not only in the political sphere but, more fundamentally in the psychology of inter-group relationships. Conflict resolution theory can be used here to shed some light on the politicisation of the paramilitaries:

If the parties can neither conquer or avoid each other, some form of procedural resolution is likely. In procedural resolution the parties have to stay together, and live with each other . . . It is almost inevitable that an element of commonness injects itself into enmity once the stage of violence yields to another relationship even though this new relation may contain a completely undiminished sum of animosity between two parties.[6]

Loyalist and republican paramilitary organisations had to make the transition from their dedication to sectarian violence to politically orientated groupings seeking to mediate an acceptable peace – the alternative was mutual annihilation. That transition and their new relationship with each other had its genesis in the prisons of Northern Ireland.

2

Political Crime and Criminalisation

The definition of what is criminal is greatly influenced by social attitudes, values and cultural belief systems, which are themselves socially
and politically determined. The definition is then enshrined in law,
which, in turn, is also socially constructed, reflecting, as it does, those
same social attitudes and opinions. In other words, the whole procedure
is a highly subjective one. This perhaps comes into sharpest focus in an
examination of 'political crime', where the 'legitimacy' of a state and its
legal system may be simultaneously under attack and defended by opposing groups in a given conflict.

Since Socrates there has been an awareness of political crime and of the
functional nature of such 'crime' in promoting social change and early
sociologists made a clear distinction between political offenders and
criminals. Émile Durkheim's anomie theory has a particular application
in Northern Ireland, where the rules and norms of civilised society dis-
integrated. Symptoms of social disintegration in the northern state can be
identified by the existence of a Special Powers Act, the introduction of
internment and the quadrupling of the prison population, the use of the
army for policing, the setting up of special Diplock courts, the award
of Special Category status for political prisoners, the implementation of
a 'criminalisation' policy, an 'Ulsterisation' policy, a 'normalisation'
policy, and so on. All of this points to a malaise within the existing
social structures, as opposed to a pathology or criminality located
within individuals.

It is generally agreed that by 'anomie' Durkheim was referring to
a state of 'normlessness' and 'social deregulation'. This occurs when a
society does not have adequate contact or interaction within its citizen-
ship to maintain the mutual understanding necessary to develop a system

of common rules and values; that in the absence of any commonality or consensus as to rules, people worked at cross purposes, uncertain of the expectations placed upon them by others, and of what they themselves could expect; the resultant confusion, inefficient performance of vital social functions and manifest discord, precipitating societal disintegration.

Durkheim's argument extended to identify crime as a normal characteristic evident in all societies at all stages of their development. He contended that a stable level of crime in society was a healthy symptom, and that only when dramatic changes in crime rates (either increases or decreases) became evident was there cause for worry. Increases due perhaps to the consensual basis or continuing legitimacy of the state being in dispute, or decreases indicating severe state repression. In either circumstance political crime can be a consequence.[1]

Durkheim further argued that crime is functional in society. As rules and norms are essential to civilised life, crime and the subsequent societal response draw attention to the necessity of the rules and the moral values underpinning them. And within this thesis he asserted that political crime could be instrumental in promoting necessary social change. In 1918 Cesare Lombroso distinguished between two categories of prisoner – 'criminals' and 'revolutionaries' or 'rebels' – and described political crime as 'a kind of crime of passion, punishable only because it involves an offence against the conservative elements of the human race'.[2]

A few years earlier, Enrico Ferri had made similar distinctions between criminal types motivated by egoism, self-gain or hostility and political offenders whom he identified as 'revolutionary or progressive abnormals ... who rebel from altruistic motives against the injustice of the present order'. However, his research led him to question the motivation of certain 'political criminals':

> Political derelicts may be committed every day, not only by man really misled by political passion (pseudo-criminal) but also by insane, born, occasional and habitual criminals, who, either by social contagion or through personal circumstances give their criminal tendencies the form of political crime. In our opinion, therefore, political criminals are either not criminals at all, or else belong to one of the five categories of the general classification.[3]

Clearly the political offender can be identified as a type, or category, but equally the criteria for eligibility to such a status is profoundly complex.

To introduce a political offender category without strict adherence to legal and social criteria is to leave such a status open to misapplication and social criticism. As Keith Bottomley comments:

> The more doubts that are expressed about the genuineness of the motivation of even just a few political criminals, the easier it becomes for those who wish to undermine the integrity of all political criminals. Once this sceptical position gains any sort of foothold, political crime as such can then be explained away and what Skolnick 1969 has called the 'riff raff theory' comes into play, whereby an entire political protest movement can be attributed to a minority of troublemakers, who are alleged to indulge in crime for its own sake and are neither genuine in their expressed motivation nor truly representative of any wider constituency.[4]

Havelock Ellis personified the political prisoner as often belonging to a victimised section in society, an oppressed minority, trying to overthrow an unjust political system or establishment, which itself may be resorting to 'criminal' methods to maintain order: 'The "political criminal" of our time or place may be the hero, martyr, saint, of another land or age.'[5]

In his analysis of crime, Willem A. Bonger identified certain crimes that were specifically against the interest of the ruling class, the class which held the power to identify what was 'criminal'. In Bonger's view, political prisoners were essentially different from ordinary criminals because they often risked life and liberty in advancing the interests of the 'oppressed classes'. As he termed it: the political offender could be viewed as 'homo nobilis', whereas the ordinary offender was 'l'homme canaille'.[6]

Obviously it may or may not be in the interests of any ruling class, or government, to give recognition to political offenders, hence extending to them credibility and legitimation. However, if such a category or status becomes necessary in a conflict situation (because only such could justify it), any refusal to recognise what is in fact political crime may of itself become a central factor in that conflict.

In conflict scenarios and large-scale sectional alienation, the ability of government to 'criminalise' political activity is called into question. In his world report on political prisoners, Lester Sobel argues:

> Critics of a government may rush to the defence of a person whom they describe as a 'political prisoner' but whom the regime denounces as a 'common criminal' ... To the imprisoned person's collaborators and

supporters, however, the alleged crimes are absolved by the political cause in which they were committed. They therefore describe the captive as a 'political prisoner' or, frequently, as a 'prisoner of war'.[7]

By introducing Special Category status in 1972, the British government recognised the political nature of the Northern Ireland conflict. The granting of what was effectively 'prisoner of war' status reflected what was the reality for loyalist and republican prisoners – they were fighting a war to determine the future of the state. The status was conceded after a prolonged hunger strike and during cease-fire negotiations with the Provisional IRA. The move was markedly out of character for the Tory administration and perhaps the decision was always viewed as a temporary measure taken in extreme circumstances.

The extent to which the government recognised the political motivation of the Special Category prisoners is nowhere more evident than in the manner in which the status was allocated. Essentially the government abdicated all responsibility for this. Once found guilty of a scheduled (terrorist type) offence, a prisoner wishing to claim Special Category status applied to the paramilitary organisation of his choice and had to satisfy it that he was either a 'member' acting under orders or that his offence qualified him for inclusion on the grounds that it was politically motivated. Individual 'cases' were considered on their merits, with the paramilitary organisations differing widely on acceptance criteria.

In general terms the organisations accepted those persons whose actions were directed against the 'enemy' in circumstances in which the prisoner was not motivated by self-gain or self-interest. Other prisoners accepted were those who satisfied the paramilitaries that they were innocent of the charges leading to their convictions. Not only had the establishment to regard a prisoner as a political offender, therefore, but the awarding of the status was subject to paramilitary ratification – a form of external validation. If a prisoner was not accepted by his chosen group he was not allocated Special Category status. The system was open to abuse in so far as there was tension between loyalists and republicans in the Long Kesh compounds. It clearly made sense to increase your strength in the compound, in case of trouble with rival compounds, and so claims for new prisoners by the respective paramilitary groups were not usually lacking, without too nice a regard for actual affiliation.

The British had taken the unprecedented step of creating a Special Category status without any legislative provision. It had been introduced under the Special Powers Act and consequently the new status had no basis in law. Prisoners who had been awarded the status had no rights and no redress in law which would safeguard their maintaining a different penal classification to ordinary criminals. When the government decided to change the rules by introducing its criminalisation policy in 1976, it was, in fact, redefining the nature of the conflict from a political conflict to criminal conspiracy. Both loyalist and republican prisoners would resist criminalisation and would suffer the consequences of defiant non-conformity in their refusal to accept the government's revised view of who and what they were.

In a criminal justice system the term 'criminalisation' refers to a process by which someone who has committed an offence becomes a 'criminal' by means of institutional criminal imprisonment.[8] Prior to the introduction of Special Category status, the paramilitaries in Northern Ireland had either experienced criminalisation in Belfast's Crumlin Road prison or had witnessed its impact upon fellow volunteers. This was a conventional prison in which paramilitary prisoners had been remanded and imprisoned, where they had seen at first hand how the criminal prison system could debase and degrade prisoners and enforce a sense of rejection. They knew that the system was capable of divesting people of all respect and self-respect, resulting in social alienation and alienation from the self, in which hatred and self-hatred become central possibilities. It is understandable, then, that they would strongly resist a measure which would return them to those conditions, and they would argue that their resistance was justifiable on political and moral grounds.

All total institutions share basic organisational features aimed at changing inmates. They are designed to reduce any sense of individuality and to promote a collective identity, with extreme dependence upon the institution and its staff.[9] On admission into conventional prison, the prisoner goes through degradation ceremonies and self-mortification rituals, as body inspections are made, and clothing and personal effects taken, to be replaced by a uniform and a number. The enforcement of psychological and physical detachments terminates tangible contact from the outside world as the prisoner is 'processed, shamed and discredited, regimented and made dependent'.[10]

The importance of the symbolic resources out of which we construct our identity is profound and has direct consequences for one's self-identity and self-perception, as was fully understood by republican and loyalist prisoners on blanket protest. In given situations, where prisoners are forced to dress identically, individuality can become difficult to assert. In effect, it can constitute a discredited basis for individual identity projection, and provokes impersonal and anonymous treatment from staff. The 'uniform' can represent a central mechanism, or device, in the process of shaming and institutional stigmatisation. (Kieran Nugent's refusal to wear 'the uniform' would mark the beginning of the blanket protest in 1976.)

Following admission, the second-stage of the reception process occurs in the wing of the prison. In the criminal regime the prisoner is 'removed' to his cell, where he waits for what is usually a calculated time for the further privations and processing that constitute the governor's interview. After the official reception procedure the prisoner initially finds himself an 'outsider' from the criminal inmate group, representing a further identity hurdle, into which he may be accepted or rejected.

During penal initiation, therefore, the prisoner is exposed to pressures from the staff and the inmates, both exerting very different sets of expectations. (In many criminal systems a prisoner may be anally raped or sexually abused by inmates as a rite of passage. This is a phenomenon which is also found in female prisons,[11] and even in some children's homes or residential units.[12])

In the conventional prison the collective prisoner rejection of administrative authority may be viewed as a threat to internal security and control – hence the official emphasis upon single cellular accommodation, restrictions upon talking or communications at work, during meals, in the corridors and wings. These restrictions are designed to break the (overt and expressive) solidarity of the criminal inmate subculture and to reinforce the prisoner's sense of rejection through the deprivation of basic rights – free movement, speech, choice, and so on. In this sense it is in the administration's interest to maximise social rejection in all areas of the prisoner's world, that he might conform willingly to its demands – on the basis of his 'worthlessness', his right to self-assertion is discounted. Such status reductions are resisted by the inmate subculture. In this context the prisoner counter-culture may be functional in protecting its membership from the ratification of rejection, through providing a strong sense of solidarity with alternative criminal value-systems, codes and norms. Furthermore, the prisoner may find that the staff culture actually complements and encourages both the criminal culture and the criminal hierarchy.

Membership of the criminal subculture brings benefits, and the inmate's 'rank' within that culture will be both recognised and respected by the prison staff. According to Clarence Schrag, the pressures upon any prisoners in such a system to join the criminal subculture and accept its values are compelling:

> The reality is simply this: the welfare of the individual inmate, to say nothing of his psychological freedom and dignity, does not importantly depend upon how much education, recreation and consultation he receives but rather depends on how he manages to live and relate with the other inmates who constitute his crucial and only meaningful world.[13]

Research has demonstrated that prison administrations are highly dependent upon the criminal inmate subculture and power structure to control prisoners and maintain the status quo. This duplicity in official standards – covert collusion and legitimation of ruthless criminal leadership – strengthens and perpetuates the status of the criminal subculture, making it more, not less, attractive to the new prisoner. Resisting membership of, and identification within, that culture would clearly carry serious consequences.

The entire basis of this interactional model is therefore dysfunctional, with inmate leadership being seized and maintained by those ruthless enough not to be challenged and who subsequently enjoy support and recognition by prison staff who are dependent upon them. As a result, in conventional criminal regimes the more extreme criminal elements rise to positions of power and benefit from an official recognition and consolidation of that power. In the words of Lloyd McCorkle: 'Prison culture is organised around the value of its most persistent and least improbable members.'[14] In short, criminality, even extreme criminality, is officially rewarded.

Perhaps the most disquieting aspect of such staff–inmate accommodations lies within their very covertness and the disparity between social expectation (informed by media, government and, for the want of a better word, officialdom) and reality. Presented with such a reality, prison staff attempts at rehabilitation and attitude modification become at best cynical, when they demonstrably support, and indeed depend upon, the criminal culture they are supposed to be reforming. Accordingly, the claim that conventional imprisonment is corrupt, dishonest and wholly dysfunctional is one that is hard to dismiss.

In a study on criminal dehumanisation and prison regimes, Philip Zimbardo undertook an experiment in the basement of Stanford University, California, in 1973. With the help of ex-prisoners, he constructed a prison approximating to the atmosphere of a real prison designed to depersonalise and dehumanise both guards and prisoners.[15] He recruited male university students through an advertisement in a local newspaper and randomly assigned them to the roles of 'correctional officers' and 'prisoners'. Zimbardo was intent upon demonstrating that, subject to such conditions, guard brutality and prisoner apathy and withdrawal would result, even though the 'prisoners' were not criminals, nor the 'guards', correctional officers – and that this was known to both groups. Due to the guards' increasing hostility toward the prisoners, who showed symptoms of psychopathology, the experiment was abandoned after only six days. As John Sabini comments:

> Whether or not this sort of brutality is a necessary consequence of prison life, the Zimbardo illustration shows in a dramatic way that features of prison life can generate extreme levels of hostility even when the inmates are not hardened criminals or troublemakers, and the guards are not self-selected for their roles by sadistic desire. The brutality was not a consequence, simply, of subjects adopting an attitude consistent with their new roles but was supported by concrete aspects of the mock prison. The dehumanisation of 'inmates' was facilitated by deprivations and mortifications found in many total institutions. Role dispossession, separation from contacts which served to validate their identities, family, friends, reference group. A requirement to wear stocking caps to detract from individualisation, i.e., presentational differentiation through hair styles, etc. Inmates addressed by prison number, not name, emphasising the enforced monolithicness of the group. A requirement to wear a uniform, in this case hospital gowns, requiring modesty in sitting or walking – a characteristic (even though necessitated by the 'uniform') regarded by both officers and inmates as feminine. Loss of autonomy and control, inmates were made to ask permission to use toilet facilities. In the event of permission being refused, a communal cell bucket had to be used.[16]

It is evident from Zimbardo's experiment that such degradations caused regression in the inmate group, which facilitated guards' treatment of them as less than human. The structural relationships of the respective groups, the disregard of individual dignity and emphasis on presentational uniformity, and general debasement, are characteristic of conventional criminal prison regimes. Yet this experiment had to be abandoned after only six days, not least because the guards' brutality was progressive. Sabini continues:

> A lesson to be learned from the Zimbardo experiment is that, although morality demands that we treat others humanely, no matter what they do, our ability to elicit humane treatment from others is a continuing accomplishment, contingent on our ability to present ourselves as humans.[17]

One of the ultimate powers that one group can impose upon another lies in the ability of the dominant group to define the identity of the subordinate group – for example, as criminal, mad and so on. This can be achieved through the mechanism of having the weaker group internalise, individually and collectively, the identity projected toward them. This was the keystone of the British government's criminalisation policy. The intention was to treat the political prisoners as criminal, to segregate them, isolate them and emphasise their criminality with an associated loss of 'rights' as 'normal' human beings. The authorities apparently took the view that if the prisoners were treated as criminal, and more significantly perhaps, labelled and evaluated as criminal, they would internalise a criminal identity. Theoretically this was fine – harsh and inhumane treatment of prisoners or patients in mental institutions can result in regression, institutionalisation and pathological personality change. Total institutions are, in the main, very effective in ensuring status passage and status transformation, in which radical changes occur in an inmates' self-evaluation. This will subsequently involve social disablement and stigma, informing how the individual is evaluated socially and in interaction with others, whether this be as criminal, strange or mad.

The underlying psychological assumption here is that over a sustained period human beings will convert total institutional rejection into self-rejection, with devastating consequences for the individual. This would have had a precise application for what the British authorities, after all, viewed as a criminal prisoner population. This reflected a fundamental official misunderstanding of the nature of the conflict in the North. Loyalist and republican prisoners were well aware of the consequences of accepting a criminal identity and many chose to protest rather than conform. Arguably this was the only appropriate response to avoid psychological 'disintegration', the central objective of criminalisation. As Gresham Sykes and M. Messenger observe:

> To this one can distinguish two basic categories of rejection. Either the prisoner shares the social rejection of himself, because he accepts with the society that punishes him that he has done something wrong, and in that case he is bound in time to crumble and he will hardly ever be what he was before – he cannot bear the continued first rejection from the community of which he feels a part; or the other type of prisoner is one who rejects society's values, or the viewpoint of the court which sentenced him, or that of the prison authorities, or even that sometimes of his fellow prisoners. Such a prisoner has a chance to avoid disintegration of his personality so long as he will go on resisting the moral pressure and accept the hardship which results from being a recalcitrant prisoner.[18]

Unlike Zimbardo's mock prison, in the real world prison officers wield very real power over individual inmates. They are in the business of man management; however, their training, education, social skills, personal disposition and cultural orientation may place them in positions to do much more harm than good. When these two groups are placed in a situation conducive to conflict, protest and resistance, the possibilities for prison officer abuses can become overwhelming.

Had Northern Ireland's political prisoners accepted criminalisation, they would have been forced, during the course of their prison sentence, into a re-evaluation of themselves as criminals, and the social stigma attaching to criminal ex-prisoners would have been a central possibility for them. This is one of the most fundamentally important (negative and characteristic) aspects of criminal imprisonment, the transformation in the prisoner's self-perception, from being normal to becoming 'discredited' (criminal). This is extremely destructive for the individual prisoner (who comes to perceive of himself as morally bad, untrustworthy, dangerous, and acts accordingly) and society, which may suffer the consequences of further offending through a reinforced disposition towards criminal activity. In short, criminalisation was introduced to ruthlessly discount and delegitimise the prisoners not only as political prisoners but as human beings. The brutalisation was meant to achieve alienation, and did achieve alienation, but this was not converted into self-rejection and internalised individually. Rather, it was managed and resisted by a prisoner collective who used the hatred generated by their physical and psychological mistreatment to galvanise the commitment to their respective causes.

The political prisoners in Northern Ireland protested against the withdrawal of Special Category status and the implementation of criminalisation, which led inexorably to the 1981 hunger strike. It is hard to fathom the British strategy in at first recognising hundreds of loyalist and republican prisoners as political prisoners and then, four years later, determining to criminalise them. One thing is clear, however, they were not inspired through any desire to resolve or lessen the level of conflict in Northern Ireland.

3

Internment and the Introduction of Special Category Status

When the Northern Ireland government introduced internment without trial on 9 August 1971, the measure was used solely against the Catholic community in an attempt to smash the IRA. In the first swoops almost 350 people were arrested, over one hundred of whom were released within forty-eight hours, a statistic which highlights the poor intelligence involved in the drawing up of the suspect list. Among those interned were community leaders and radical activists. Their removal, it has been argued, created an excellent opportunity for the 'hard men' to fill the gap, men who had been prudent enough to ensure they did not have a high public profile. The measure, and the selective way it was implemented, intensified Catholic grievance and sense of injustice and led to an escalation of violence:

> It was followed by riots, gun battles, heavy casualties and the intimidation of about 2,500 families from their homes during that month ... And the Provisionals' campaign continued with even greater violence. There is little doubt that internment and the interrogation methods used by the army and police hardened minority opinion and assisted the Provisionals.[1]

Internment was a special form of imprisonment which operated outside the constraints of the conventional criminal judicial system. People were interned without due process on suspicion of political or paramilitary activity levelled against the state, in circumstances where evidence did not exist or could not be obtained for normal judicial proceedings. Their arrests were made by the army, not the police, and involved subsequent detention without redress to normal courts or appeals procedures, and they were held in compounds rather than cells, in a penal regime which had few characteristics of ordinary prisons. At first the internees had been placed in the already overcrowded Crumlin Road prison or in the equally unsatisfactory conditions of the prison ship *Maidstone*, which had been brought to Belfast Lough from Britain. However, in September 1971, the 'republican' internees, then numbering some five hundred men, were sent to Long Kesh, a new high-security prison with fenced compounds and Nissan hut accommodation.

Regardless of the nature of the arrests and internment, the government and the Prison Service were reluctant to consider internees as political prisoners. It was argued, however, that by introducing internment in response to civil disturbance, the political motivation of 'offenders' who could not be dealt with through the usual criminal justice procedures had, in fact, been conceded.[2]

The subsequent treatment of internees in the Long Kesh compounds also departed radically from the traditional treatment of prisoners in conventional prisons. For example, rehabilitative and social work interventions were not considered appropriate or practical for the internees. Such treatment assumes the innate 'sickness', or pathology, of the prisoner and this approach was considered irrelevant for men caught up in a political social conflict. A further difference existed with regard to the high security treatment of internees which involved large numbers of armed troops guarding the perimeter of the camp, watchtowers, regular helicopter surveillance, and so on. In total, the conditions under which internees were imprisoned approximated a World War II prisoner-of-war camp. The manifestly different rationale of internment vis-à-vis 'ordinary' crime and criminal justice procedures raised complex issues which, in the end, were not addressed and which would have profound implications for the status of the prisoners.

The unconventional treatment of internees created an interesting anomaly in the status of those who were interned on suspicion of politically motivated offences and those who had been convicted of the same type of offences prior to 9 August 1971. Between September 1971 and June 1972 the Crumlin Road prison confined many paramilitary prisoners who also claimed to be political prisoners but who had been processed and integrated in the prison system as 'ordinary criminal' offenders. In June 1972 Special Category status was awarded to these convicted prisoners.

The decision to introduce Special Category status did not involve par-
liamentary debate or consultation with Northern Ireland political parties
or the Northern Ireland Civil Service. It took the form of political executive action. Tim Pat Coogan has described the circumstances surrounding the introduction of this category as being akin to a 'cloak and dagger'
affair,[3] a view which is borne out by the absence of any serious research or
literary investigation or debate into the matter, given that this status was
central to both the management of prisoners and of how the conflict
would be defined.

Clearly there were a number of factors which combined to make the
introduction of Special Category status a shrewd political move. As
already stated, it redressed the anomaly of treatment between those
interned on suspicion of paramilitary involvement and those sentenced
as a consequence of it. It brought an end to a hunger strike embarked
upon by republican and loyalist prisoners and a work strike by loyalist
prisoners, all of whom were protesting for political status. The deaths of
republican hunger strikers could have led to a serious escalation in violence both in the prison and elsewhere. In such circumstances the political
gamble with the Provisional IRA – political status for cease-fire – must
have represented an attractive option in the face of apparently insur-
mountable prison difficulties. It immediately eased tension in Belfast's
Crumlin Road prison, the only male prison in Northern Ireland at the
time, where gross overcrowding was making conditions untenable,
with paramilitary prisoners virtually beyond the control of staff, seriously risking staff and intergroup security. (By 1972 the state's prisoner
population had increased to 1,117, compared to 727 in 1968. This
number excludes internees.) Most significant, however, was the decision
of Secretary of State William Whitelaw to negotiate with the Provisional
IRA, which stipulated that political status for its prisoners was a precondi-
tion for peace talks. The most substantial contact between the British and
the Provisionals occurred on 7 July 1972 at a secret meeting in London
between William Whitelaw and a top level Provisional IRA delegation.
(IRA leaders were flown from Belfast to Oxfordshire by RAF Andover.)
Whitelaw's concession to their demand was strategic.[4]

However, when the government introduced Special Category status it
insisted that it did not constitute *political* status. But as Billy McKee, the
Provisional IRA's officer commanding (OC) in the Crumlin Road prison,
commented, 'We didn't mind what they called it; we knew what it

was.' A cease-fire was declared on 26 June and the talks began, but the British Army, among others, questioned the wisdom of such a strategy:

> There was a division of opinion on the British side, however, as to the wisdom of these talks. The military and in particular the GOC Northern Ireland, General Harry Tuzo, received the news with outrage, and the demeanour of some of the civil servants, with whom the Provisionals had dealings, was not exactly welcoming either.[5]

The army's principal concern was that Special Category status gave the IRA further legitimation as a military and political entity.

The strategic negotiations proved unsuccessful. On 9 July the Provisionals called off their truce, having secured Special Category status – as Paddy Hillyard later commented, 'violence may determine penal policy not only in the immediate present but for years to come'.[6] The Provisionals' decision to resume violence is explained by Tim Pat Coogan:

> For their part, the British gave an impression of condescension and heartlessness that repelled the IRA – 'Whitelaw is a ruthless bastard.' 'We can accept the casualties,' he said, 'we probably lose as many soldiers in accidents in Germany'; that sort of philosophy, which was not confined to Whitelaw, was a major factor in the IRA decision to have a bombing campaign in England – where the casualties would not be 'acceptable'.[7]

The ramifications of a new prison classification had implications at a number of levels, involving radically revised treatment of prisoners, limiting the power of prison staff, extending through to the strategic management of the Northern Ireland conflict. The fact that such fundamental issues were not addressed at the highest levels, political and professional, suggests an abuse of executive power. That Special Category status actually constituted a better form of imprisonment was a matter of fortune rather than a policy informed by psychological and criminological analysis.

The British had introduced a 'humane containment' form of imprisonment, which did not institutionalise, dehumanise, criminalise or alienate prisoners, but afforded them a degree of dignity and liberty, unknown and without precedent in recent British history. The compound system allowed men to survive prison relatively intact, both psychologically and emotionally, with a degree of self-respect and functional autonomy which would have been impossible in conventional British prison systems. As from 22 June 1972 Special Category prisoners were granted the same concessions as their internee counterparts:

1 One visit per week
2 One food parcel per week
3 Unlimited incoming and outgoing mail
4 The right to wear personal clothing at all times
5 Free association with other prisoners
6 No statutory requirement to engage in prison work

The Special Category system provided the opportunity for virtual inmate group autonomy, group responsibility and vastly increased possibilities for self-determination, all within the confines of penal containment. The system put into practice the philosophy that Winston Churchill had somewhat optimistically expressed – that prisoners were sent to prison as their punishment, not to be further punished.

Compound Structure and Organisation

Long Kesh, a former army base, had been prepared under emergency conditions and conformed to a prisoner-of-war-camp model. The surrounding countryside is bleak with a flat terrain offering little cover, the landscape dominated by high watchtowers with mounted searchlights. It was, indeed, essentially a prison camp, with an adjoining army camp, surrounded by a wide perimeter of barbed wire and high, corrugated iron boundary fences. As a prison, therefore, Long Kesh was very different in origin and organisation to any conventional civil prison in the United Kingdom when the five hundred internees arrived in September 1971.

As from December 1972, Long Kesh saw the transfer of convicted prisoners from Crumlin Road prison, a move which greatly alleviated the pressure in that prison. Within one month approximately 60 loyalist and 170 republican Special Category prisoners were relocated in Long Kesh. (About forty ordinary criminal offenders were also accommodated in the prison at that time and were housed in Portakabin-type huts located a discreet distance from the compounds. These low-security prisoners were used to 'service' the prison with cooking, delivery and site cleaning duties.) By 1974, for security, administrative and classification purposes, there were five recognised paramilitary groups in the compounds:

1   Ulster Volunteer Force (UVF): loyalist
2   Ulster Defence Association (UDA): loyalist
3   Provisional Irish Republican Army (PIRA): republican
4   Official Irish Republican Army (OIRA): republican
5   Irish Republican Socialist Party (IRSP): republican

Within these groupings there were members of other paramilitary organisations. The UVF, for example, accommodated the Red Hand Commandos, and the UDA accommodated the Ulster Freedom Fighters, both of which are arguably more militant than their host organisations. However, it would be difficult to separate out all the factions within the five recognised groups; generally the subgroupings were able to integrate without overt conflicts.

As discussed in chapter 2, the allocation of Special Category status to a prisoner was in practical terms an issue determined, or at least ratified, by the respective paramilitary groups. Any prisoner wanting to make application for the status usually did so shortly after arrest. The decision to accept (or not) was determined by the relevant paramilitary OC in the prison, in liaison with his organisation on the outside.

Broadly speaking, those who qualified for consideration and acceptance were either paramilitary members acting under orders or non-members charged with:

1   Possession of firearms or explosives for personal safety, area
    defence, or offence against 'the enemy'
2   Those accused of membership of a proscribed organisation
3   Involvement in riots and street fighting
4   Approved offensive actions
5   Fringe activities, including providing 'safe houses' for the use of
    paramilitaries on the run, and so on
6   Those wrongfully convicted of terrorist crimes.

The Provisionals claimed non-members whom they felt sympathetic towards and actual membership of their organisation was not a condition of acceptance for Special Category status. Similarly, the UDA accepted non-members into their compounds during the time of their imprisonment. These individuals were not obliged to retain membership on completion of their sentence, the UDA taking the view that co-opted or conscripted members are more of a liability to the organisation than an asset when returned to the community. The UVF, on the other hand, did not accept non-members into their compounds. This procedure and these considerations again provide a stark contrast to any conventional UK penal processes.

Each compound normally consisted of four separate Nissan huts, with a separate shower and latrine unit, and measured approximately 80 × 80 yards, bordered by high-wire security fences – in effect, forming a large cage.

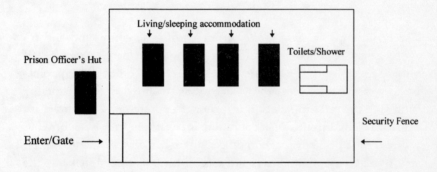

A compound contained some eighty men, living in close proximity and interacting on a fairly intensive basis. The accommodation provided in the Nissan huts was basic – bunk bedding, sleeping areas partitioned by hardboard, a central corridor for meals and, given constraints upon space, limited area for recreational activity. The prisoners were in control of day-to-day activities within their own compounds; however, prison staff had free access to patrol, search, lock and unlock individual huts morning and evening. Patrols of varying duration were carried out on a daily basis, and compound searches (some highly extensive) according to the governor's discretion were undertaken to maintain the security of the prison. Therefore, while there was a very high level of prisoner autonomy, the prison was still effectively under the control of the Prison Service.

Food was delivered to the compound entrances by lorry, having been prepared in the prison's central kitchen. The large metal containers were collected and distributed by the prisoners. Accordingly, prison staff were not involved in the time-consuming chore of food distribution. In addition to institutional food (a source of complaint and even riot in some prisons), each prisoner received a weekly food parcel from family and friends, and there were small cookers in the compounds upon which personal rations could be prepared. This arrangement constituted a major contribution to the quality of life in the closed world of the prison.

There were many similarities in the prison command structures in each of the paramilitary organisations. Where differences do exist, however, they tend to be important, as can be demonstrated by examining the largest three organisations – PIRA, UVF and UDA.

PIRA

The Provisional OC was elected from within the compound and his appointment is subject to ratification by the movement's brigade staff outside the prison. The second-in-command and other staff appointments were determined by the OC according to knowledge and expertise relative to the posts in question. A prisoner in possession of a university degree or a diploma in higher education, for example, may be an obvious choice for the post of education officer, an ex-bank clerk, finance officer, and so on. Compound officers and specialists (line officers) make up the next level of command and are also elected from within each compound. It is evident from this organisational structure that the Provisionals developed a hierarchical command system, with an advisory, or staff level, supplementing an executive of line officers. The structure successfully encourages consensual involvement and compliance at volunteer level.

UVF

The UVF operated a more autocratic command structure, with no elections and with officers in control of appointments. Although some time after this part of my study ended in 1979, power and command were seized from the existing officers.

UDA

The UDA operated the most flexible and democratic system. All appointments to the 'officer' ranks were by election from within the compounds, with the exception of the second-in-command, who was selected by the OC. The UDA OC's responsibilities extend to administration, welfare, negotiations with the prison administration and contact with the external organisation. Anyone, at any time, could put himself forward for election to OC, and provided he had serious support and credibility from the outset, and the necessary votes at ballot, he could assume command. (Significantly during the five-year period 1974–9 there were only two OCs appointed, the former commander having been released.) Apart from officer elections, prisoners stood for election to serve on various committees – sports, education, security and entertainment. Prisoners who were elected onto these committees were invariably those with particular aptitude or interests in the areas described.

Non-members were treated by PIRA as civilians, and were excluded from organisation meetings, et cetera. The UVF insisted upon membership of the organisation, not making provision for any other category of prisoner. The UDA treated non-members on equal terms, not excluding them from any aspect of compound life.

Each compound had a quartermaster who took responsibility for all items other than personal belongings. His role was to maintain a complete inventory of tables, chairs, utensils, bedding, et cetera, and to obtain replacements where necessary, either through the prison stores or from the external organisation. His responsibilities extended to 'quality control' of prison food and the monitoring of all incoming personal parcels.

A compound administrator was responsible for all requests made to see the prison governor and professional staff – medical, dental, welfare and education – recording the nature of requests, frequency of visits and, as appropriate, monitoring progress, and ensuring a close control of prisoners' contacts with the 'prison world external to the compound'.

A welfare officer was also appointed in each compound to deal with prisoners' marital, social or family problems. This was a particularly sensitive appointment, inevitably involving utmost confidentiality. By and large, the more routine and trivial matters were collated and referred to the prison's social work department via the compound welfare officer. His responsibilities included dealing with enquiries about a relative's progress if in hospital, enquiries about inadequate social security payments, arranging for extra visits or extensions of visiting time on welfare grounds. Generally this form of self-help was encouraged by social work staff, on the understanding that individual prisoners had freedom of access to their department about private or confidential matters. This liaison with paramilitary welfare services was extremely well developed, including a minibus transport network for visits from all parts of Northern Ireland, practical support for prisoners' wives and dependants, providing for both social contact and material assistance, often in circumstances where social services were unable or unwilling to help.

Compound welfare officers were generally very aware of their limitations in dealing with prisoners who had complex personal difficulties. The more serious cases were referred directly to the social work department. These included severe marital problems – estrangement, breakdown, reconciliation – and difficulties in adjusting to long sentences, personality/identity crises, coping with a relative's terminal illness, and family difficulties arising from absence of the father, such as truancy and loss of confidence, which often led to complex negotiations with social services, lawyers and social security departments on behalf of the family.

The education officer in each compound was responsible for all library requests. His role included interviewing prisoners wanting to commence classes, undertake O and A level courses, Open University and correspondence courses, ensuring that these limited facilities were not abused. He also took up any prisoners' complaints with the prison's education officer, regarding teaching content in courses, and the availability of materials, books, and so on.

The internal organisation and administration of the compounds demonstrated a very high degree of independence and autonomy, obviating the need for extensive and intensive prison staff involvement. The most important common denominator in all the paramilitary organisations was their strong military ethos. The organisational structures in themselves, therefore, served as a daily reminder of why the men were in prison, as volunteers of their chosen group, fighting for their cause. (Interestingly, during a lengthy period of this part of my study most of the OCs had served with the British Army.) The proximity of 'enemy' organisations also served to reinforce the perception of being prisoners of war and not criminals.

As a result, Special Category prisoners were largely self-disciplined and self-governing within their compounds, and were virtually insulated from prison staff, which had two central advantages:

1   Inmates were not humiliated, debased, labelled, stigmatised,

processed – in short, made to feel less than human (in Zimbardo's terms) or 'criminalised'.[8]

2 The role of prison guards was structurally determined and clarified. Depending upon the personal disposition of the guard, and the ethos and rationale of the prison regime, this can vary from a supervising and befriending role at one extreme (treatment orientation) to a humiliating and brutalising role at the other (punitive orientation). This potential for role ambivalence and variation was resolved in the compound system, where prison officers' responsibilities toward prisoners was confined to guarding, escorting, searching, given mutually imposed constraints upon interaction and 'relationship' formation. The role of prison officers as carriers of institutional culture, labellers, stigmatisers, processors, agents of expressive societal rejection was consequently minimised. This carries an enormous significance which will be comprehensively analysed in Part Two of this book.

The atmosphere within the compounds was consensual, liberal and permissive, and underwritten by the fact that volunteers could leave their compounds by approaching prison staff at an opportune time and electing to be removed to the conventional section of the prison. (In my experience a very limited number of men resorted to this option.) The staff attached to each compound operated from a small wooden hut or, at times, a caravan, referred to as 'the bunk', offering very basic accommodation. These bunks were located at compound entrances, and all movement in or out was monitored. However, as Gusty Spence recalled:

> The day-to-day life of the prisoners within each compound is organised and controlled not by prison staff, but by the prisoners themselves according to the group to which they belong. Each of the groupings, Provo, Officials, UVF and UDA have their own indigenous identities and run their compounds differently.[9]

It has been observed that a relaxation in staff control can actually make for less freedom in prison life:

> Where staff permissiveness includes non-surveillance, it may simply create a power vacuum which the more prisonized components of the inmate population will fill. Inmate surveillance replaces staff

surveillance, and inmate life may become less permissive in terms of
the freedom available to choose between alternative modes of
behaviour.[10]

The fact that this did not happen in Long Kesh again points up the differences between criminal offenders and political offenders in terms of social
organisation in confinement. Special Category prisoners were, given
their structural organisation, enabled to approximate 'normal' life style
in prison (within the limitation of penal constraints) in an environment
characterised by consensus, relatively free from the dehumanising, debas-
ing and (socially) alienating processes endemic in conventional regimes.

These conditions were overtly recognised by the administration. In
return for realms of autonomy prisoners assumed responsibility for discipline and self-control, resulting in comparatively negligible incidents of
rule-breaking (one of the main criteria in measuring the success of any
prison system). As a result the staff role was revised from one of supervision and discipline to one of general security, which radically reduced
the officer–prisoner ratio.

The psychological and interpersonal implications of compound imprisonment vis-à-vis conventional imprisonment are extremely significant. The most critical difference between the two systems lay in the
structurally restricted staff–prisoner interaction of the compound
system. Prison staff did not have the power over, or access to, prisoners
to humiliate, demean, or otherwise to institutionally reconstruct their
identities from 'normal' to 'criminal'. Consequently, the alienation
experienced in conventional regimes was almost completely avoided in
the compound system, and this was massively beneficial for the individual prisoner, and ultimately for society at large.

4

Common Ground in Long Kesh

Soldiers engaged in war may at times have more in common with the enemy than with the governments or peoples who will them to fight. It is fairly simple – you either develop a respect for the enemy shooting at you, or you die. It is the basic psychology of war. It is perhaps only in close combat that we see ourselves in the faces of those who would kill us, and only then do we understand that we share in equal measure our humanity and inhumanity, the goodness and the 'shadow'.[1] When we recognise this in ourselves, and see it in our enemies, enmity tempered with empathy becomes a real possibility. This was certainly the outcome for the political prisoners of the warring factions in the Northern Ireland conflict. If prison is, as it is often argued to be, a microcosm of society, this retrospective study of Long Kesh gives some cause for optimism, albeit tinged with the bitter disappointment of an opportunity missed.

Atrocities carried out against Protestant and Catholic communities by republican and loyalist paramilitaries throw the divisions in the North into sharpest focus. It would seem, then, that of all the groups in Northern Ireland, these, the paramilitaries, would be the last to become reconciled. None the less, from 1974 to 1976, loyalists and republicans achieved such a degree of accommodation in the compounds of Long Kesh that it could reasonably be described as the forerunner of the peace process announced some twenty years later. During this period, despite – or perhaps because of – deteriorating conditions in the wider community, there were particularly favourable circumstances within the prison perimeter for achieving intergroup relationships between the opposing paramilitary prisoners.

The extent of sectarian division[2] and segregation[3] in Northern Ireland, especially in working-class ghettos where life is lived almost exclusively in the company of co-religionists, has been well documented. In exceptional cases, where relationship possibilities exist across the religious divide, family and peer group condemnation often ensure they do not continue. Given a separate existence and an absence of intergroup interaction, one community has virtually no first-hand experience of the other. For many paramilitaries, then, it was Long Kesh, with its prisoner-of-war-camp conditions, that provided the first opportunity of direct contact with people from a different religious and political background. Given that all the five main paramilitary groups actively fighting in the North had members in local prisons, under the 'control' of a highly pressurised Prison Service, intergroup accommodation was inevitable. It was inevitable precisely because the very survival of the respective prisoner groups depended upon it.

The first political prisoners, or those who were to attain Special Category status, including Gusty Spence, were incarcerated in 1966 after the murder of a Catholic barman in Malvern Street in the loyalist Shankill Road, Belfast.[4] The loyalists convicted for the murder, after a controversial trial, were imprisoned in A Wing, Crumlin Road prison. A Wing was the prison's long-term section, housing men serving sentences of three years or more. The first sentenced republican prisoners were members of the Provisional IRA who were sent to Crumlin Road prison in December 1970. Official IRA prisoners were sent to the prison in the summer of 1971 at a time when the two IRA factions were engaged in a violent feud. As it was too dangerous to place OIRA prisoners in PIRA cells, the loyalists agreed both to accommodate them, and to protect them.

The administrative policy of Crumlin Road prison during that period was one of non-segregation, and loyalists, Officials and Provisionals shared the cellular accommodation of A Wing, which had communal dining and working facilities. The Officials' cells were in the loyalist section of the wing, with the loyalist cells providing a buffer between the two republican groups. The atmosphere in the prison during that period was extremely tense and the prisoners, particularly the Officials, regarded their personal safety to be at risk. However, the prison authorities took the view that segregating the various factions would have been tantamount to special treatment and they insisted upon handling the inmates as ordinary prisoners.[5]

The first serious incident between the factions occurred in the winter of 1971 when loyalists and Provisionals began fighting in the prison's dining hall. The fight was broken up quickly and only a few minor injuries were sustained. However, it did serve to illustrate plainly enough the inherent dangers of the situation. Faced with the administration's intractability regarding segregation, the paramilitary OCs took the initiative and agreed to a 'no-conflict' policy to avert the repetition and escalation of conflict.[6]

The political prisoners in Crumlin Road prison were among the most extreme members of the paramilitary groups in Northern Ireland. Their proximity and relative accessibility to each other could have meant annihilation of the weakest inmates or weaker groups. Certainly the Prison Service would not have had the capacity to intervene with any significant impact, indeed their intervention may have drawn hostility from all sides. The no-conflict policy was, therefore, evidence that the respective paramilitaries had formed relationships because of the very conflict in which they were engaged. The motivation of the relationship was a defensive one – to minimise risk. In terms of relationship formation stages, this development was one of antagonistic co-operation – a minimum starting point. As G. Simmel states in relation to conflict resolution processes:

> If ... there is any consideration, any limit to violence, there already exists a socialising factor, even though only as the qualification of violence. Kant said that every way in which the belligerents do not impose some restrictions in the use of possible means upon one another necessarily ... becomes a war of extermination.[7]

The conflict between the paramilitaries was, therefore, the common element through which was established the basis for mutually agreed regulations and norms between men representative of the most alienated sections of their respective communities.

Each OC took responsibility for his men's behaviour toward other groups and individuals. Hence, prisoners were accountable primarily to their own officers and not to prison staff. In effect, the administration's insistence upon non-segregation exposed prisoners to a degree of risk which required the intervention of their own paramilitary leaders, to secure non-aggressive intergroup behaviour. It is important to emphasise that these prisoners were not conforming to prison rules when they regulated their behaviour; rather, they were adhering to rules laid down by their own leaders. The ethos of their conformity was accordingly transformed from 'alienatively', as it would have been in response to the directives and sanctions of prison staff, to 'normative'.

It was not until Special Category status was introduced in 1972 that effective segregation of loyalists and republican prisoners took place in Crumlin Road prison. In November 1972 Gusty Spence, OC of the UVF, was the first sentenced Special Category prisoner to be transferred from Crumlin Road to Long Kesh. At that time ordinary criminal prisoners and Special Category remand prisoners were accommodated in Long Kesh. The Special Category remand prisoners occupied two compounds, one for loyalist prisoners and one for republican prisoners.

While the compounds were segregated, the visiting area and medical welfare facilities were shared, and fighting between the groups was common. The respective paramilitary leaders, who had access to each other 'at the wire' of the compounds, or in medical welfare waiting rooms, agreed that the fighting should stop, and they formed a 'non-aggression pact', which constituted the first step toward interfactional, or paramilitary, 'working relationships' in Long Kesh.

On 10 December 1972 approximately sixty sentenced loyalist Special Category prisoners were transferred from the Crumlin Road prison to Long Kesh. The following week a similar number of Official IRA Special Category prisoners were also transferred, and after Christmas over one hundred Special Category Provisional IRA men were transferred. These Special Category prisoners occupied four compounds in close proximity, two Provisional IRA, one Official IRA and one loyalist (UVF and UDA mixed).

From 1972 until 1974 the numbers of Special Category prisoners in Long Kesh increased dramatically and by March 1974 some eleven compounds (approximately 1,200 men) were occupied by remand prisoners and sentenced Special Category prisoners. (Long Kesh also held some 600 internees; there were 7 republican internee compounds and one loyalist.) These Special Category prisoners were divided into two areas of the prison known as 'phases', phase five and six. Phase five was predominantly loyalist, housing three loyalist compounds and two republican (one OIRA/IRSP and one PIRA). Phase six was predominantly republican, with five PIRA compounds, and one UVF. The OCs of the UDA, UVF, PIRA and OIRA were held at phase six and direct communications between all the senior officers were easily arranged. Contact between phase five and six was facilitated through a centrally located football/exercise area. The visiting area was also shared by prisoners from both phases, and the prison tuck shop was located in phase five, which meant that the OCs could legitimately visit that area for provisions.

In March 1974 a Provisional IRA remand prisoner escaped from the 'waiting area' (where prisoners waited to see their visitors). The administration responded by introducing more stringent security measures. Prior to the escape, the visiting cubicles consisted of small rooms flanked on either side by access corridors, visitors entering from one side, inmates from the opposite entrance. For the duration of the visit the doors were closed, which allowed for a degree of privacy and intimacy, although staff could observe through a glass panel fifteen inches square.

In April 1974, as a consequence of the escape, doors were removed from the cubicles, leaving them fully open for visual and audible observation. Small tables in the cubicles were extended wall to wall, dividing the room and preventing close physical contact. These alterations represented a fairly drastic change for the prisoners. The loyalists and republican OCs formed a 'camp council' to consider a unified response to this new, enforced arrangement.

For approximately fourteen weeks no Special Category prisoners requested or received visits from families or friends. Tensions, which were predictably high in the camp, were reflected in the wider community, with loyalist and republican militants hijacking vehicles, burning buses, and blocking roads, in a demonstration of solidarity with the Long Kesh prisoners. This served to illustrate, tangibly enough, that Long Kesh was not a closed institution in the conventional sense, but rather a prison in which prisoners could enlist direct and militant support in the community outside. Before calling off their protest the camp OCs were not only assured of improvements in the visiting arrangements but were invited to inspect modifications in the cubicles, which had restored them to their former state, allowing for both privacy and intimacy. When the camp council called off its protest visiting recommenced.

For the first time loyalist and republican paramilitaries had negotiated and taken co-ordinated action in a common cause. This significant development was much underpublicised despite the importance of its implications. In relationship terms, they moved to a further stage − beyond self-defence.

August 1974 saw the beginning of a food protest in Long Kesh. The original complaint emanated from a loyalist compound and concerned both the quantity and the quality of prison food. When this was raised at the camp council all the groups expressed dissatisfaction with the food and also with the laundry arrangements (sheets and pillowcases were laundered monthly). The camp council informed the prison administration of the prisoners' grievances, warning that if improvements were not forthcoming food would be thrown 'over the wire'. Later that month, in a show of solidarity, all loyalist and republican paramilitary groups draped sheets and pillowcases over the perimeter fences of the compounds and commenced throwing prison food rations over the fencing onto the road outside.

On 9 September the following statement was issued by the Northern Ireland Office: 'No sentenced or remand prisoners in the Maze Prison [the government renamed the prison in 1974] will be permitted to receive food parcels from their relatives, or be allowed to purchase food from the camp shop.'[8] Prison food continued to be thrown over the wire. On 14 September Secretary of State Merlyn Rees, in a statement to the press, promised improvements in both food and laundry facilities.

On 17 September Special Category prisoners in Magilligan prison in County Derry began their own food protest in solidarity with the Long Kesh inmates. In both prisons food was being thrown over the wire and sheets were draped over compound fences, preventing the authorities from observing what was going on inside, which created an eerie, abnormal and deeply threatening atmosphere in the prison.

The internees in Long Kesh were not involved in the food protest and did not have any restrictions imposed upon their food parcels. The next development was one of the most striking examples of intergroup cooperation in the compounds. Known as the 'Ho Chi Min trail', all Special Category prisoners and internees made ropes from wire, cord and clothing and devised a pulley system to transport food from compound to compound. High vantage points were selected in each of the compounds and ropes were lined up between them, often covering considerable distances. When all the compounds were connected to the pulley system the internees began sending cigarettes and fresh provisions – meat, fruit, vegetables – to the Special Category prisoners. The authorities looked on open-mouthed as supplies changed hands by the ingenious overhead transport network.

This degree of accommodation and reciprocity between hardline loyalists and republicans constituted another significant development which had a profoundly beneficial effect upon intergroup relationships within the prison. The external paramilitary organisations found it difficult to understand what was happening in Long Kesh, as certainly they had experienced no comparable accommodations between each other beyond the prison perimeter.

On 23 September the Special Category prisoners were given assurances about an improvement in the quality of food and the loyalists decided to terminate their protest but the republicans opted to carry on. The loyalists were allowed to receive food parcels and use the prison tuck shop from that date, and they continued to supply the protesting republicans with food, a course of action which highlighted the strength of the intergroup relationship. Loyalists were prepared to give up supplies in order to sustain that relationship.

When the food protest finally ended, the administration agreed to allow the paramilitary OCs access to any compound in which members of their organisation were contained. There was some disparity in the interpretation of this 'privilege'. The loyalists understood that this applied only when stable conditions prevailed in the camp. The Provisionals, however, took it to mean that the OCs had permission to see their men in order to prevent escalations in tense or troubled situations. In the event, the difference in interpretation was to have considerable importance.

By September 1974 Long Kesh had had a troubled three-year history. One of the most contentious factors during that period was the use of British troops in searching internee compounds which led to many allegations of mistreatment and brutality. On 29 September an escape tunnel was found in one of the republican internee compounds and the Provisionals alleged that prison officers physically assaulted prisoners in retaliation. This was regarded by the Provisional OC as a further provocation in an already unacceptable situation. In a statement to the press the Provisionals threatened to burn all the prisons in Northern Ireland, 'unless beating of defenceless men stopped'.

On 15 October the Provisional leader of compound 13 asked for the removal of a prison officer from his compound. The Provisionals maintained that the officer had been involved in the mistreatment of republican internees. This procedure was used when individual prison officers were deemed by the prisoners as 'unacceptable' and consequently the compound leader could not vouch for his safety. In this instance the prison officer concerned refused to leave and was assaulted by the prisoners. The administration asked for those responsible to be handed over so that the authorities could instigate the appropriate disciplinary procedure. The compound leader refused to comply with the directive and the administration responded by stating that the army would be brought in to seize the prisoner who had been mainly responsible for the assault.

By early evening the OC of the Provisional IRA was aware of the situation in compound 13. Accordingly he requested to see his officer in that compound. The request was refused, as were the second and final requests. By 9.30 p.m. British Army troops began to mass at the perimeter of compound 13. On the Provisional OC's order to 'burn the camp', the sentenced Provisional prisoners set fire to their compounds in the top section of the prison. Upon seeing the flames, the Provisional internees followed suit and the Official IRA also joined in the protest. The loyalists did not take part in the burning of Long Kesh and for security reasons, in the midst of what was to be a battle, assembled in strength in compounds 14 and 19, after breaking down the fence gates of their compounds. Prior to this evacuation, however, loyalist prisoners had successfully raided the prison hospital, taking an abundance of medical supplies which they thought they would need for themselves. During the short-lived confrontation between Provisional IRA/Official IRA and the army, loyalists rescued many republican prisoners and set up field hospitals in compounds 14 and 19.

That evening all the Nissan huts in Long Kesh were razed to the ground, with the exception of those in compounds 14 and 19 which were held by loyalists. As dawn broke, British troops moved in. The Provisionals and Officials faced superior numbers, CS gas and rubber bullets, and in the words of one UVF prisoner, 'it was no contest'. The UVF OC had observed the 'battle' from a vantage point, and upon realising that the republicans' position was untenable, approached the British Army officer in charge and attempted to secure from him an assurance that if the republican prisoners returned to their compounds peacefully, no further offensive action would be taken against them. The UVF OC was then allowed to see the Provisional OC, who in turn ordered his men to return to their compounds; the Officials followed suit.

Once again the conflict in Long Kesh precipitated violence in the community, demonstrating the very close inter-relationship between the prisoners and their host communities. On 17 October the *Irish Press* reported:

> In Belfast, there was widespread hijacking and several confrontations between the army and IRA gunmen. Barricades were erected in republican ghettos and bus services were suspended in all areas of Belfast except for the strongly Protestant East Belfast.[9]

Trouble spread to the three other prisons in Northern Ireland. The *Irish News* reported that

> in Armagh, Ulster's only prison for females, the inmates took the Governor and three prison officers hostage and claimed that they would hold the hostages 'until our men are safe, and we know they are safe'. The hostages were later released through the instructions of the Long Kesh Provisional CO.
>
> In Magilligan, the administrative offices and kitchens were set on fire, as Republican prisoners there demonstrated solidarity with their counterparts in Long Kesh.[10]

And according to the *News Letter*:

> In Londonderry, demonstrators forced the withdrawal of bus services and all shops closed by lunch time. Protests and high-jackings also occurred in Newry and elsewhere in the Province.[11]

There was an obvious lesson in this. Long Kesh was unique among British penal institutions at that time as it contained a prisoner population which was powerful enough to enlist direct outside support in response to coercive actions taken against it. The prisoners had established themselves as a potent group, through their organisations' support and public support, and had successfully brought pressure to bear on an administration unused to being made accountable for its actions.

The accommodation processes which took place in Long Kesh were made easier through the presence of a common enemy – the prison administration. However, the alliances which were formed developed into something much more significant than prisoner collusion. There were advantages in taking unified protest action, but there were also risks in terms of outside group support, especially in the loyalist sector where such alliances could be viewed as betrayal. These processes and periods of united action between the paramilitary groups had latent consequences and potentials which the camp council recognised and endeavoured to exploit. In the first instance, this was to involve attempts to advance the general welfare of the prisoners they represented.

The Downtown Office

By the end of 1974, then, the membership of the camp council had found common ground with one another. Terrorists from violently opposing traditions discovered that they could live together, co-operatively, and even agree to distribute food and rations upon the basis of need. The existence of this bonding between the groups was subsequently known to the community at large – as this 1978 *News Letter* report indicates:

> Talks at Camp Council level over matters of common interest to all factions has led to a healthy mutual respect between leaders of all the five paramilitary groups held there. Outside the Maze, meetings between the paramilitaries do occur, but from time to time only and largely because of the 'bond' that has been struck up during the years of imprisonment – there is no Republican/Loyalist hot line but a sort of underground grapevine which may be used to check bona fides.[12]

There was agreement that the transposition of their relationship within the camp council to the outside would be of benefit to all the groups, if only at a welfare/sharing of common interests level.

Welfare (through-care and after-care) had always been one of the main topics on the camp council's agenda and was clearly important to all the organisations involved. The paramilitaries wanted a support base on the outside which would involve their own welfare groups and prison welfare officers, as they knew and trusted the personnel involved. In June 1975 David Morley, the Provisional IRA OC in Long Kesh, drew up a document in which he proposed an 'Outline Scheme for Resettlement'. This document was to be the basis of future negotiation upon which the paramilitaries bargained for an effective prisoner after-care scheme. It called for the establishment of a central office in Belfast to be controlled by the prison welfare service, as 'they have the confidence of both the prisoner and the voluntary groups'. An important aspect of the scheme lay in the proposed co-ordinating committee, in which voluntary, probation and prisoner welfare groups would be represented. This committee, therefore, with prison welfare service involvement, would structurally provide for interaction between the welfare wings of the five main paramilitary organisations in the North. Designed to advance welfare issues, the clear political potential could not be ignored. In effect, the paramilitaries in Long Kesh wanted a central 'downtown office' to be located in Belfast and made available to prison welfare officers, with the support and involvement of loyalist and republican welfare organisations.

The loyalist prisoners submitted their document – 'Proposals for a Resettlement Programme'. This outlined in considerable detail the many problems besetting a prisoner and his family, both financially and emotionally, during and after prolonged periods of imprisonment. In the short term, they suggested that 'a central office be set up primarily in "downtown" Belfast under the management of an "accepted welfare officer". This office could be used as a base where the representatives of the various Prisoners' Welfare bodies could meet, discuss and work for the common welfare of all prisoners.'

The two documents were submitted to the camp council for consideration. The council, embracing representatives from PIRA, UVF, UDA, OIRA and IRSP, deliberated and agreed to the following submission for the consideration of the Northern Ireland Office:

1 The service provided by the statutory prison welfare units enjoys the confidence of all prisoners and the value of the work being done by them is fully recognised and appreciated. The considerable extent to which prison welfare officers have managed to co-operate and co-ordinate their effort with the work of the voluntary prison welfare organisations is also recognised and it is appreciated that this has made possible the more effective use of resources.

2 That the Prison Welfare Service is part of the Probation Service is understood as is the concept of through-care by a single service responsible from when a person is committed to prison until he or she is able to resume normal life in the community. It is acknowledged that such a service can only be provided when it is voluntarily sought and it is on this basis that the prison welfare service operates.

   i The setting-up and staffing of an office in central Belfast to cater for the welfare and resettlement needs of prisoners in providing a place to which the families of prisoners, others interested in their welfare and discharged prisoners themselves could resort. The office, in fact, would be a suite of offices housing a probation office, a voluntary welfare office, a conference room and a waiting room. Within these offices could be fostered the relationships which we all desire, and which for too long have been absent. There would be an immediate identification with this office and concern for prisoners and dependants. A blend of the trained and untrained could take place without hyper-sensitivity, each recognising the other's role in society; the professional and the voluntary.

ii   The improvement of the service provided for those in custody by liaison with prison welfare officers, probation officers working in the community and voluntary agencies. Encouragement could be given to the voluntary bodies by the Probation Service, and advice tendered where and when necessary.

iii   The identification and analysis of problems of discharged prisoners seeking help and advice and an endeavour to find solutions to them, either by intervention by staff in charge of the central office or the appropriate welfare agency.

iv   The co-ordination of the work of the voluntary prison welfare organisations (close to the paramilitary groups) by arranging meetings of their representatives to discuss matters of common concern affecting prisoners' welfare and resettlement where appropriate, the taking of concerted action on their behalf.

Conclusion

3   Prompt and decisive action is demanded because the whole problem of prisoners, their dependants and the resettlement of ex-prisoners has gone on for too long.

The Long Kesh Prison Welfare Unit senior officer, Elizabeth Kennedy, was a resolute woman of remarkable courage. She and another welfare officer had been heavily involved in fostering

paramilitary negotiation. However, this closed and potentially dangerous world was somewhat beyond the remit of conventional probation
practice. The prison welfare officers' integrity was accepted and recognised by all the paramilitary groups. They had secretly volunteered their
services to facilitate the downtown office proposal, their involvement
known only to the senior level of the imprisoned paramilitary community. There would not have been the remotest chance of the mainstream probation and after-care service countenancing the involvement
of its officers (seconded as prison welfare officers to the prison) in such a
politically charged scheme. Accordingly, the extent of the prison welfare
officers' involvement in this process was, and remains, a closed book.

The atmosphere in Long Kesh at that time was electrifying. In effect a
political forum was being proposed, under the guise of a prisoners'
welfare service, which could have led to an increasing and reinforcing
dialogue between the warring factions. It was seen by most of those
involved as a potential road to peace – something to be cherished, nur-
tured, and fully resourced and facilitated in its evolution. That the paramilitary leaderships in the prison wished to transpose the process they had
been engaged in to the wider community was the stuff of history.

The downtown office idea was potentially a high-risk, high-gain
venture for the groups concerned. In the event, the paramilitary leadership inside Long Kesh was strong enough in terms of support and
capability to maintain and foster relationships with the 'opposition'.
Common ground and consensus did begin to evolve in the prison to an
extent where all the leaders wanted the opportunity to set up channels of
dialogue between paramilitary welfare groups in the community. The
downtown office would have provided a means toward achieving this
goal.

Ostensibly, the downtown office would have had a function of providing a through-care and after-care centre for prisoners and their
families, involving the welfare groups of all the organisations, with professional social work support. From the outset it was agreed that the office
would help all prisoners and their dependants, and that there was no
question of an exclusive service for Special Category prisoners. At
another level the downtown office would have provided a channel for
contact and communication between the various personnel of the paramilitary welfare groups, which would have been mutually supportive,
providing for republican/loyalist paramilitary interaction. This was seen

as highly important in symbolic terms, grass roots members seeing and being exposed to members of opposing organisations, even in a welfare capacity, knowing and relating to the 'opposition' in conjunction with professional specialist social workers.

Only if this operation were successful would the third level of the scheme come into effect. The developmental logic was, where one had a degree of communication and co-operation at welfare group level, the path would have been open for the creation of a forum which would have been the nucleus for dialogue and exchanges of views between the paramilitaries. The forum could have been operated in the same way as the camp council in an enlarged form and would have initially required its supervision.

Given the political vacuum which existed in Northern Ireland at that time, the downtown office had important integrative potential. A political initiative by the paramilitaries would have represented a formidable threat to the political establishment for two reasons. First, a paramilitary leadership by its nature is a working-class leadership, which would have presented a challenge to élite and privileged groups on both sides. Second, and more importantly, a paramilitary-controlled downtown office would have represented the beginnings of a cross-community alliance which, if developed, could have challenged the whole social structure of Northern Ireland. However, the extent of such developments would have been carefully controlled by the paramilitary groups, who were well aware of their political limitations.

While the downtown office talks in Long Kesh were largely secret, subsequent dialogue between loyalist and republican representatives provoked an interesting, if predictable, response from the political establishment. In May 1977 the *Irish News* reported:

> A warning that moves to get agreement on a Northern Ireland solution between the Provisional IRA and the Loyalist paramilitary organisations was 'giving status and dignity to murderers' came yesterday from Dr Conor Cruise O'Brien, Minister for Posts and Telegraphs.[13]

In the same month the *News Letter* reported:

> Mr Ian Paisley's Democratic Unionist Party said, 'As far as we are concerned, we have only one message for the IRA – we seek their annihilation!' A spokesman added, 'We consider any arrangement with the IRA bombers and gunmen as surrender to Ulster's bitterest foes. The DUP believes that peace and stability can only be achieved through the

military defeat of the IRA.'

The leader of the Official Unionist Party, Mr Harry West, said, 'Any such discussions are completely repugnant to us. We are not going to have two sorts of gunmen running the country.'

The Ulster Special Constabulary Association said, 'The "secret meetings" could lead the Province into total anarchy.'[14]

Given the political stalemate and intractability which existed in Northern Ireland at that time, the paramilitary groups appeared to have a greater freedom and range of options with which to reach consensus or even resolution. As Sarah Nelson writes in her article 'The Ulster independence debate':

> One reason why paramilitaries felt freer to toy with such dangerous new ideas than politicians was they did not have to keep looking over their shoulders at the electorate and at other groups contending for the voter's support. Another reason was that some militants were more prepared than other people in the population to contemplate a form of settlement which accommodated and consulted 'the extremes'. The conviction that they had been doing the 'real' fighting for their country and deserved consultation about the future encouraged limited fellow feeling with, and understanding for, the IRA [this was especially true of loyalist prisoners]. Thus, while Loyalist politicians were still talking of the need to defeat the IRA, people like McKeague [loyalist paramilitary leader] were openly admitting that one attraction of independence was its accommodation of the Provo's anti-British aspirations. They did not see such an accommodation as appeasement but rather as political realism.[15]

In 1974 the loyalist and republican paramilitaries were equally suspicious about the sincerity of a British involvement in what was potentially *their* peace process. All the paramilitary groups felt that they could be manipulated and exploited by British self-interest.

In March of that year Merlyn Rees became Labour's Secretary of State for Northern Ireland. Within days he appointed Stan Orme, a strong critic of the unionists, as Minister of State. The previous Christmas the Provisional IRA had claimed that they were in receipt of a message from the British to the effect that 'HMG wished to devise structures of disengagement from Ireland'.[16] There is no doubt that the British had withdrawal on the agenda and that plans were in place to facilitate such a development. According to Paul Bew and Gordon Gillespie, 'Merlyn

Rees admitted afterwards in a letter to the London *Times* in July 1983 that a cabinet subcommittee dealing with Ireland had "seriously considered withdrawal".'[17] The British withdrawal policy was frustrated by several developments, the most significant being an escalation in loyalist paramilitary attacks on the Catholic community,[18] and the fact that Dublin insisted that a British withdrawal 'must not be contemplated'.[19] Not surprisingly the Irish government did not relish the prospect of having to engage a Protestant army in the North.

As Minister of State, Stan Orme was the government representative who was to become involved in peace negotiations with the camp council in Long Kesh.[20] A government White Paper published in 1975 stated:

> In recent months various groups within the community have shown an increased desire to participate in the political process and a growing belief that they can best find for themselves political relationships which will be acceptable to them. The Government believes it is essential that participation in this process should take place not only between like-minded groups but equally between groups which hold apparently strongly opposed views.[21]

While any prospect of peace would have been good news for the majority in the North, it could be argued that it would not have been such good news for a British administration 'seriously considering' a withdrawal from Northern Ireland. Peace in the North carried the consequence of an expensive continuing British involvement in the region. The British attitude to the talks was described as 'high-handed', and 'out of touch with reality'. Some of the participants felt as if they 'were talked to like children'. Although the British had stated that the paramilitary groups could reach political accommodations 'for themselves', they now proposed a British civil service saturation in the talks. Negotiations between the paramilitary groups would have been highly sensitive, and for some, highly dangerous. (At that time there were loyalists who, without hesitation, would have killed their co-religionists for talking to the IRA.)

In the end it was British attitudes and British demands which ensured the termination of the talks and the potential to develop any peace process. They did not just miss the opportunity to establish a peace forum between the paramilitary groups, they destroyed it. Within months of holding political negotiations with the paramilitary leaderships in Long Kesh, the government announced its intention to end Special Category status and to introduce 'criminalisation'. Initially this aroused more protest with loyalists than republicans, not because they objected to a change of status for their prisoners but because they believed that 'a British withdrawal was just around the corner in any event'.[22] In June 1975, John Whale had written in the *Sunday Times*: 'The retreat from Ulster is on, and it's working. An epic change is being accomplished in Britain's relationship with Northern Ireland. British withdrawal is becoming a fact ... The British Government has triumphantly completed that part of the necessary psychiatric therapy which consists in alienating the patient's affections.' If the government was intent upon alienating a section of the Northern Ireland people, they were certainly going to achieve it, but not in the form Whale anticipated.

In phasing out Special Category status the British Government was ending a form of imprisonment that had allowed for political and social accommodations between the paramilitary groups. This had led directly to dialogue, and a desire for further dialogue, among the paramilitary groups. Instead of fostering this initiative, the government committed itself to criminalising the political prisoners in Northern Ireland, in a calculated act of provocation against the paramilitaries. There was nothing new in this – they were replicating the policy used in the south of Ireland which had facilitated a British withdrawal in 1921. Criminalisation, prisoner protests and hunger strikes had fuelled nationalist alienation, produced martyrs and provided militant republicans with an unprecedented groundswell of support. And there were more recent indicators as to how republicans would respond to criminalisation: Billy McKee's hunger strike for political status in Belfast's Crumlin Road in 1972; Seán Mac Stiofáin's hunger strike in the Republic in 1972 (there were fears of 'open fighting in the South if Mac Stiofáin died');[23] the Price sisters' hunger strike in 1974, which 'force feeding had ended after 167 days';[24] Michael Gaughan's hunger strike and death in Parkhurst Prison in June 1974; Frank Stagg's hunger strike and death in Wakefield Prison in February 1976, which resulted in rioting in Belfast and bombing in Derry. But, nevertheless, the British continued in their policy to criminalise the entire republican movement's prisoner population, supported by unionist politicians who appeared to welcome any repressive penal measures taken against the prisoners. While loyalist political prisoners would also be subject to criminalisation and resent its implementation, the prison conflict was to be essentially between the British and the IRA. The writing was on the wall for those who could see.

5

The End of Special Category Status

By 1975–6 almost all Northern Ireland's political prisoners had Special Category status. In the compounds of Long Kesh they were experiencing the benefits of a humane system of imprisonment, one which had significant and substantial advantages over any criminal, or criminalising, conventional form of criminal imprisonment.[1] This system had been providing favourable conditions for contact communication (and even conflict resolution) between the paramilitary groups which could not have been achieved in 'normal' circumstances in the community. During this period there was no serious social, political or pressure group demands for repressive changes in the Northern Ireland prison system. Both the loyalist and republican communities had very substantial numbers of their young men in prison, almost in equal numbers. Then, suddenly, in 1976 the government announced its intention to phase out Special Category status and the compound system and to put into place a new criminalisation policy. The consequences would be dire – the loyalists, in particular, believed 'that Northern Ireland was in for a roller coaster ride of conflict escalation' and began to make contingency plans for all eventualities, including a British withdrawal. A leading loyalist commented at that time, 'There won't be many of us left standing, after this one's over.'[2]

Criminalisation was an unmitigated disaster in conflict resolution terms, in that it brought Northern Ireland perilously close to civil war during and after the 1981 hunger strikes. It also was a distasteful and repugnant policy from criminological, psychological and sociological perspectives. In 1979 government had been advised of the criminological and conflict management advantages of the compound system, and of the likely consequences of imposing a criminalisation policy which would be met with prisoner resistance to be acted out in the H-Blocks of Long Kesh.[3]

Conventional imprisonment does not protect society from further crime; instead it releases prisoners who have become alienated and highly motivated to re-offend. Criminologist Edwin H. Sutherland has observed that their motivation to re-offend springs largely from a desire to exact revenge on the society which countenanced their excessive punishment.[4] That a government would introduce criminalisation as a conscious and deliberate policy with any prisoner population is fairly alarming in its own right. That a government would attempt to criminalise a population which it had already recognised as a special category is incomprehensible in criminological terms. This would suggest that government policy intended to turn (de facto) political prisoners into criminals, criminals with access to guns, explosives, training, organisation, logistics, and so on, for if criminalisation had had the desired effect on political prisoners in Northern Ireland, the consequence would have been political and social anarchy. Criminalised armed factions with quasi-military capability would have produced levels of crime and insurrection which had not been seen in the North. And society in general would have been held responsible for the inhumane treatment and punishment of the prisoners. The community would pay the price.

Fortuitously, neither the prisoners nor their host communities would accept that their 'volunteers' were criminal. This alone, perhaps, was to prevent a decline into anarchy in Northern Ireland. After March 1976 all sentenced 'political prisoners' – those who would have previously qualified for Special Category status – were sent to the new H-Blocks. Special Category prisoners in the compounds were offered (unspecified) favourable early release consideration if they volunteered to transfer to the H-Blocks as conforming prisoners. Only a small number of men elected for this option, as it effectively involved a renunciation of political prisoner status.

On 15 September 1976 Kieran Nugent became the first republican prisoner to protest for Special Category status. On his refusal to wear a prison uniform he was not given alternative clothing, so he wrapped himself in a blanket.[5] Henceforth all such protesters were dubbed 'blanket men'. Republican political prisoners were ordered not to wear a prison uniform or take part in prison work by the brigade staff of the Provisional IRA. By May 1977 almost 400 republican prisoners and approximately 20 loyalist prisoners were engaged in this form of protest. The importance which the Special Category prisoners, and those aspiring to such status, placed upon the right to personal clothing is not without significance, the prison uniform representing as it does a mechanism for stigmatising and discrediting a prisoner. When the Provisional IRA issued a statement regarding the proposed phasing out of Special Category status they were very clear on this issue:

> Already volunteers of Oglaigh na hEireann have been instructed that they are not to engage in any institutional schemes under the control of the prison administration. They are further instructed that they are not to wear any clothing provided by the prison administration, even if such clothes are of a civilian type.[6]

The protest was a contentious issue within loyalism. Unlike the huge numbers of republican prisoners 'on the blanket', supporting and sustaining each other, the loyalist blanket men were a minority who endured the privations of that protest largely unsupported, morally or practically. They felt badly let down by their fellow loyalist prisoners in the 'conforming' H-Blocks, but they were supported by the loyalist prisoners in the compounds. Both UDA and UVF protesters also felt themselves to be comparatively abandoned by their external organisations. But they were political prisoners and they had the courage of their convictions to assert that fact, with or without wider loyalist support. The loyalist blanket men held the view that if all loyalist prisoners had gone on the blanket, the government would have delivered concessions. As one former prisoner put it:

> In the last analysis all the prison officers live in loyalist areas. If they were seen to be taking repressive measures against all loyalist prisoners, the pressures upon them would have been intolerable. The government would either have made concessions, or would have had to move all the screws, their families, and their extended families, into the prisons. The loyalist paramilitaries run all loyalist areas.[7]

During 1978 a majority of loyalist political prisoners in the H-Blocks went on blanket protest, and maintained the protest for a number of weeks. However, the OC of one of the loyalist factions took his men 'off the blanket', and the other groups had little choice but to end their protest also. The loyalist commander could not have realised the significance of his actions. Concessions would, indeed, have been forthcoming in the face of a joint (but distinct and separate) loyalist and republican protest action. The hunger strikes, and all that went with them, could have been avoided.

It was perhaps understandable why more loyalist prisoners did not embark upon protest action. Many were hypersensitive to being seen to join forces with the IRA. Some took the view that they were in British prisons, and as British citizens, they were obliged to obey the rules. Others felt reluctant to get into a conflict with prison officers, knowing that (usually Protestant and loyalist) prison officers and their families could 'suffer' as a consequence.

These valid reasons explain why more loyalist political prisoners did not join in the protests, but they should not obscure the fact that it would have been in the loyalists' long-term interest to have acted collectively with the republicans. Their action could even have saved the lives of the eighteen prison officers who were destined to die as members of a Prison Service which was implementing criminalisation policy. The reality was that there was going to be a very heavy price to pay for the barbarity and inhumanity of treatment which would drive republican prisoners into the dirty protest, hunger strikes and death. It would be the loyalist and Protestant community which would substantially pay that price.

There can be little doubt that the government wanted to escalate the protest at the earliest opportunity – it responded swiftly by depriving protesting prisoners of all privileges. Because of their refusal to wear prison uniforms, the prisoners were punished through 24-hour lock-up, loss of all 50 per cent remission, and deprived of exercise, free association, reading material, books, radio, television and recreation. (In the administration's determination to maximise the prisoners' deprivation, even salt, pepper and jam would become construed as 'privileges'.) The question of whether fresh air, exercise and free association were privileges or rights was to become a central issue.

By January 1979 republican and loyalist protesting prisoners had endured the deprivations and privations associated with their resistance for over two years. These conditions of inhumanity and degradation were presided over by an apparently cynical, indifferent and unfeeling British government. On New Year's Day Bishop Cahal B. Daly dramatically interceded on behalf of the prisoners, republican and loyalist alike. He issued the following statement:

... The first thing to say about this situation is that men are suffering; men are suffering terrible degradation, in inhuman conditions. Their families and friends are suffering with them and for them. No matter what explanation or justification is given for this situation, and no matter how responsibility for it may be said to rest with the prisoners themselves, it must be declared that it is folly to refuse to review the situation which allows prisoners to continue indefinitely living in such conditions. No matter how the blame for the situation is apportioned, these conditions are objectively in conflict with all recognised codes governing the environment in which prisoners are to be allowed to live. These conditions are in contradiction with all enlightened contemporary penology.[8]

Rumblings of discontent were also emanating from some quarters of the Northern Ireland Prison Service, a service not usually noted for its progressiveness or humanitarianism. There were officers who were appalled by the brutality associated with criminalisation policy. Later that year the *Sunday News* reported that

> most of Northern Ireland's 2,800 prison officers will today be deciding whether or not to sign up with a new wardens' representative body which intends pushing for sweeping changes in the way the Province's penal law is applied.
>
> For the men behind the move claim current Northern Ireland Office policies on prisons are putting officers and prisoners at each other's throats and making no attempt at rehabilitation.
>
> The new Progressive Prison Officers Committee ... has also accused the Government here of forcing officers to subject prisoners to a 'brutalising and intolerable way of life ... This is leading to a tremendous feeling of frustration among ordinary officers and is also putting us on the front line. We are being looked upon as expendable' ...
>
> 'Most of us don't have the qualities and capabilities needed for working with human beings in what are inhuman conditions – for both staff and inmates,' added one officer.[9]

There is an important point to be made in relation to this statement. It is all too easy to blame prison officers for the inhumane conditions in the H-Blocks of Long Kesh. As demonstrated in the Zimbardo experiment, even under favourable conditions role play approximations of prison life involves regression in 'inmates' and inhumanity and brutality in 'guards'. When prisoners defiantly protest, hostility inevitably increases between the prisoners and the guards and the situation becomes a potentially dangerous configuration. If you then remove the means for the prisoner 'to present as human', remove his clothing, offer him a prison uniform which you know he will not wear, leaving him naked and vulnerable, you create the conditions which are conducive to in-humane and brutal treatment. Individual prison officers were not to blame for this. They had become ensnared in a pathological institutional configuration which was a consequence of the introduction and manage-ment of criminalisation policy.

Almost two years before the hunger strikes, the potential existed for a dangerous intensification of the prison crisis and this was obvious to anyone involved with Long Kesh at that time. This was a situation which should not have developed, which should have been subject to negotiation and resolved, even if minor concessions had to be made. Prison managers and prison psychologists must have realised the conse-quences of allowing such institutional conflict to intensify. But in the last analysis it was the government's responsibility. The loyalists were not involved in the 'dirty protest', in which prisoners smeared excreta on their cell walls; however, it was to have a particular impact upon some of them. There was often a difference in how loyalist and republican pris-oners were treated by the prison officers – the brutality inflicted on the republicans was more extreme. Republican protesting prisoners were at their most vulnerable when leaving their cells to slop out, as they would become open to abuse and assault (as witnessed by loyalist political pris-oners). As a result, they began throwing the contents of their toilet con-tainers out of their cell windows. When the windows were blocked, they resorted to leaving the overflowing containers on the cell floor. The pris-oners then decided to escalate their protest by smearing excreta on the cell walls. (The mistreatment of prisoners which led to such extreme action will be discussed at length in Part Two.) To anyone on the outside the extremity of that protest and conflict may be difficult to understand. As discussed, a deeply abnormal and pathological situation had been allowed to develop, and this carried abnormal and pathological consequences. The conditions in the protesting wings of Long Kesh were virtually beyond human comprehension by August 1978. Again it was the Catholic Church which felt morally obliged to bring this to the attention of the British government. Cardinal Tomás Ó Fiaich, Primate of All Ireland, reported after visiting prisoners, including protesting prisoners and those involved in the dirty protest:

Having spent the whole of Sunday in prison, I was shocked by the inhuman conditions prevailing in H Blocks 3, 4 and 5, where over 300 prisoners are incarcerated. The prisoners' cells are without beds, chairs or tables. They sleep on mattresses on the floor and in some cases I noticed that these were quite wet. They have no covering except a towel or blanket, no books, newspapers or reading material except the Bible, even religious magazines have been banned since my last visit.[10] No pens or writing materials, no TV or radio, no hobbies or handicrafts, no exercise or recreation. They are locked in their cells for almost the whole of every day and some of them have been in this condition for more than a year and a half.

The fact that a man refuses to wear prison uniform or to do prison work should not entail the loss of physical exercise, association with his fellow prisoners or contact with the outside world. These are basic human needs for physical and mental health, not privileges to be granted or withheld as rewards or punishments. To deprive anyone of them over a long period – irrespective of what led to the deprivation in the first place – is surely a grave injustice and cannot be justified in any circumstances. The human dignity of every prisoner must be respected regardless of his creed, colour or political viewpoint, and regardless of what crimes he has been charged with. I would make the same plea on behalf of Loyalist prisoners, but since I was not permitted to speak to any of them, despite a request to do so, I cannot say for certain what their present condition is.

Several prisoners complained to me of beatings, of verbal abuse, of additional punishments (in cold cells without even a mattress) for making complaints, and of degrading searches carried out on the most intimate parts of their naked bodies. Of course, I have no way of verifying these allegations, but they were numerous.

In the circumstances I was surprised that the morale of the prisoners was high. From talking to them it is evident that they intend to continue their protest indefinitely and it seems they prefer to face death rather than submit to being classed as criminals.

The authorities refuse to admit that these prisoners are in a different category from the ordinary prisoners, yet everything about their trials and family background indicates that they are different. They were sentenced by special courts without juries. The vast majority were convicted on allegedly voluntary confessions obtained in circumstances which are now placed under grave suspicion by the recent report of Amnesty International. Many are very youthful and come from families which had never been in trouble with the law, though they lived in areas which suffered discrimination in housing and jobs. How can one explain the jump in the prison population of Northern Ireland from 500 to 3,000 unless a new type of prisoner has emerged?

The problem of these prisoners is one of the great obstacles to peace in our community. As long as it continues it will be a potent cause of resentment in the prisoners themselves, breeding frustration among their relatives and friends and leading to bitterness between the prisoners and the prison staff. It is only sowing the seeds to future conflict.

Pending the full resolution of the deadlock, I feel it essential to urge that everything required by the normal man to maintain his physical and mental health and to live a life which is tolerably human should be restored to these prisoners without delay.[11]

This statement was clearly based upon a deeply compassionate response to the prison conditions which Ó Fiaich encountered. In it he conveyed his view, to the British government, that hunger strikes were inevitable if concessions were not made. At that time all the government had to do was to give the prisoners their own clothes, which were already held in the prison. His words of concern were appreciated by many of the loyalists.

The moral indignation expressed by such a prominent figure as Ó Fiaich not only strengthened the resolve of republicans and nationalists in Northern Ireland, but crucially rallied opinion abroad as well. In Europe and in Britain it created sympathy for the republicans. Those who had taken a neutral stance were now roused by the human rights issues highlighted by the dirty protest. In America considerable attention was given to the H-Block crisis by the Irish Caucus and other pro-republican groups, and an increase in funding was sent to Ireland by the Irish-Americans. (This flow of funds had almost dried up through the efforts of Irish and British ministers touring America, condemning the activities of paramilitaries in the North.) As well as new allies, the H-Block protest produced new recruits, resources and arms for the republican paramilitaries.

The British would be seen as the unfeeling oppressors of the nationalists and republicans by a whole new generation of Irish Catholics, some of whom would dedicate themselves to 'removing the British presence from Ireland'. On the other hand, the British would continue to blame the prisoners for the crisis, even though the brutality, inhumanity and degradation were entirely their responsibility and were a direct result of their prison policy. The loyalist blanket men were deeply shocked by the barbarity and inhumanity of their treatment during the protests. One loyalist former prisoner wondered how the republicans 'were able to take even worse treatment in their stride'. The answer was simple, it was what they had expected.

6

Hunger Strike

The management of the prison issue and the increasingly inhumane treatment of prisoners had an inevitable outcome, a republican hunger strike. In October 1980, seven prisoners – six PIRA and one INLA – began to fast in support of their demands for the right to wear their own clothes and be excused prison work. By mid-December Sean McKenna, a PIRA prisoner, was close to death and with negotiations under way between prisoners and the administration, the strike ended. However, relations broke down and on 1 March 1981 – the fifth anniversary of the phasing out of Special Category status – Bobby Sands, the leader of the PIRA prisoners, began his fast 'unto death'. On 5 May he was the first hunger striker to die – nine others were to follow him.

The long time spent enduring the brutal subhuman conditions of the blanket protest and the dirty protest had increased both the hunger strikers' conviction and their resolve. According to one loyalist life sentence prisoner:

> They simply had no choice, they couldn't have gone on under those conditions. They were driven to hunger strikes. They would have been better off dead, than living like that. And given the hell they had been through for four years, there was no question of surrender, to wear the criminal uniform. Not after that.[1]

Interventions by Cardinal Ó Fiaich to secure some concessions were ignored, as were his warnings to the government that their 'management' of the prison crisis was 'risking the wrath of the whole nationalist people'.

Francis Hughes died within one week of Sands's death. The *Irish News* reported:

As Francis Hughes became the second hunger striker to die in the Maze Prison just a week after the death of Bobby Sands the Taoiseach Mr Charles Haughey declared that 'no Irish government can be indifferent to the prospect of those deaths continuing'.

The tragic events of recent weeks have confirmed once more that Northern Ireland, as it is presently constituted, is no longer a viable entity. A new political arrangement is the only way forward to peace.[2]

The events in the H-Blocks were carrying consequences which were so serious they were causing a major reconceptualisation of Northern Ireland's position within the United Kingdom. The point had been reached where events in Long Kesh were central not only to the conflict, but to the broader political entity of the state itself. The correlation between tension in the prison and tension in the community outside was again being demonstrated. Everyone waited for the Provisionals to act:

[Francis Hughes's] death raises the question of whether the Provisional IRA will now attempt to launch a full-scale offensive. Something of this kind had been expected following the death of Mr Sands, but it failed to materialise, the Provisionals apparently preferring to hold their hand as pressure mounted on the British Government to alter its attitude to the H Block protest.[3]

Riots broke out after every death and polarisation was at its height:

'Let the dirty bastards die', freshly painted in the Donegall Road sums up the Protestant feeling. 'We're sick of watching the wrecking and the burning on television,' says John McMichael of the Ulster Defence Association ... Catholic anger increases with every Catholic death, whether it is in the Maze or in the streets of Belfast. There the most tragic victim last week was Julie Livingstone who died as security forces were dealing with reaction to Hughes' death.[4]

The atmosphere surrounding the May district council elections was highly charged:

What these elections will show is which candidates can claim to speak for the Protestants, and which for the Catholics. It is a sad reflection on Northern Ireland politics that I find fewer candidates who speak for both than there were in 1977 ... Catholic support for the Provos is undoubtedly growing as the hunger strikers die and some moderate Catholics are predicting that the Government may soon find itself in a repetition of the 1916 uprising when the rebels achieved really popular support.[5]

British policy in Northern Ireland's prisons was stimulating further alienation within the state, a development which could only benefit the aspirations of the Provisional IRA.

On 21 May a third hunger striker, Raymond McCreesh, died. On 24 May the *Sunday Independent* warned: 'Already Government policy has provided the IRA with its greatest influx of recruits since Bloody Sunday and has left some sections of our youth so alienated that they no longer pay much attention to the denunciations of violence.'[6] And at the end of the month the *Sunday Times* commented:

> The deaths on hunger strike, the funerals, the riots, burnings, murders and intimidation, receive a passing mention in the cliché-ridden statements to the 'hear hears' of the equally detached members on both sides of the House ... If Britain were deliberately intent on making matters worse to prolong its disastrous tenure of direct rule, or misrule, the decision not to postpone the local government elections to a less fevered time could not have been bettered. The swing to extremism was perfectly predictable to everyone ...[7]

The criminalisation policy precipitated a political and conflict scenario powerful enough to force a reconsideration as to the desirability or even the feasibility of maintaining the British presence in Northern Ireland. In April 1981 an editorial in the popular British daily newspaper, the *Daily Mirror*, stated:

> So long as Ulster is patrolled by British troops, policed under British authority, financed by British taxpayers and controlled by British politicians the troubles will continue.
>
> The only solution must be an Irish solution. That requires Britain to withdraw from Ulster – troops, money and all – and leave the Irish to settle their future among themselves.[8]

The true nature of the British political disposition towards Northern Ireland has always been in question. As expressed by Ian Paisley, 'We don't believe that there is the will to defeat the IRA as far as the British Government is concerned, for the government has the same aim as the IRA – a united Ireland.'[9] Or as Padraig O'Malley comments on a more insightful and incisive level:

> Of course, even if Britain would like to sever the link with Northern Ireland despite the objections of a majority there, she could not publicly acknowledge the fact. And thus her dilemma: because both Protestants

and Catholics accept that she could not acknowledge such intentions, they dismiss, for their own reasons, her public statements to the contrary.[10]

The tactical *coup de maître* of the criminalisation strategy lay in the fact that it was fully endorsed by unionists and some loyalists, because it was seen to be directed primarily against the IRA. The British government, given its public pronouncements of commitment to Northern Ireland, was clearly not free to openly initiate a policy change. Rather, circumstances propitious to a British withdrawal had to be created – they would have to be seen to be forced out, to have had no reasonable choice. It was only in such circumstances that they could abandon the Protestant North with honour. If the British government had been preparing for a constitutional change in the status of Northern Ireland, the protest against criminalisation policy and the resultant hunger strike had secured massive support in Britain, Europe and America. On 31 May 1981, by which time four hunger strikers had starved to death, the *Sunday Press* listed the government's options accordingly:

1 Complete independence for Northern Ireland – probably impractical, just on economic reasons alone.
2 Devolution from Westminster – could work only in the unlikely event of Protestants agreeing to share power with Catholics.
3 Joint sovereignty – a new concept under which Northern Ireland would be governed from London and Dublin through a joint legislative council to oversee a Stormont Parliament (Northern Ireland citizens would have dual nationality).
4 British withdrawal and Irish reunification.[11]

Criminalisation and the resultant increase in the conflict achieved by that policy was in fact creating political possibilities that would have been unthinkable in conditions of peace and social stability. Ironically, however, the Provisionals confounded any plans by the British to withdraw in a most unlikely way. They responded to the deaths of their men on hunger strike not with a series of 'spectaculars', as the loyalists expected, but with a new political strategy. (While on hunger strike, Bobby Sands had won the Fermanagh–South Tyrone seat in the April 1981 by-election. He died a month later.) No doubt there were divisions and disagreements between the military and political wings of the

Provisional IRA. The political wing apparently won through at the end of the day. No one, however, could have anticipated that the Provisional IRA, placed under the most extreme provocation, would respond to the deaths of its prisoners with political tactics.

In the emotionally charged and ominous atmosphere pervading the hunger-strike period, there is little doubt that a militant Provisional response would have precipitated loyalist paramilitary actions. In such circumstances an alienated British public would have been unlikely to tolerate their government's previous level of involvement, which would in turn have become a catalyst for change, absolving governmental commitment. As Padraig O'Malley comments:

> After ten years of stalemate, owing in a large measure to intractable Protestant intransigence on the question of power sharing, the British public has grown increasingly disillusioned with Northern Ireland and increasingly receptive to thinking in terms of 'Ireland's Irish problem'. In times of austerity and record unemployment, the financial cost to the British taxpayer is becoming both enormous and unbearable.[12]

During the hunger strikes the *Sunday Times* undertook research to determine the attitudes on British withdrawal of some 64 newspapers in 25 countries throughout the world. It found that

> out of 64 foreign newspapers 59 said that Britain should withdraw unconditionally from Ulster, and take steps to secure reunification. Only 5 said that Britain should remain in Ulster and keep the peace. Only one newspaper gave unconditional support to Mrs Thatcher. There was consensus amongst editors that the deaths of the hunger strikers had improved the image of the Provisional IRA.[13]

The sense of vulnerability and isolation within loyalism was now even stronger. In 1981 Northern Ireland was on the brink of war and the loyalist paramilitaries were preparing for the worst. The Provisionals must have understood that an escalation of their war would have drawn loyalist fire, which, in turn, they would have had to respond to, in a conflict scenario which could have rapidly run out of control. They may have reasoned, however, that it was the British, and not the loyalists, who were their primary enemy. The loyalists were not responsible for the hunger strikes – they had also protested against criminalisation. It may be the case that the Provisionals, with maturity and wisdom, decided against the anticipated escalation in violence in order to avoid full-scale war.

Notes to Part One

Chapter 1

1 Steve Bruce, *The Red Hand: Protestant Paramilitaries and the Northern Ireland Conflict*, Oxford University Press, 1992, p. 18
2 J. Bowyer Bell, *The Irish Troubles: A Generation of Violence 1967–1992*, Gill and Macmillan, 1994, p. 177
3 *Loyalist News*, August 1971
4 J. Cusack and H. McDonald, *UVF: For God and Ulster*, Poolbeg, Dublin, 1997, p. 102
5 D. Boulton, *The UVF 1966–1973, An Anatomy of a Loyalist Rebellion*, Torc Books, Dublin, 1973, p. 153
6 Quoted in K.E. Boulding. *Conflict and Defence, General Theory*, Harper and Law, New York, 1963, pp. 309–10

Chapter 2

1 Émile Durkheim, *Division of Labour in Society*, Free Press of Glencoe, New York, 1964, pp. 353–73
2 Cesare Lombroso, *Crime, its Causes and Remedies*, Little Brown, Boston, 1918, p. 226
3 Enrico Ferri, *The Positive School of Criminology*, C.H. Kerr, Chicago, 1913, p. 78
4 A.K. Bottomley, *Criminology in Focus*, M. Robertson and Co., Oxford, 1979, p. 17
5 Havelock Ellis, *The Criminal*, 3rd ed., Walter Scott, London, p. 1
6 W.A. Bonger, *Criminality and Economic Conditions*, Little Brown, Boston, 1916, pp. 378–80
7 Lester Sobel, *Political Prisoners, A World Report*, Facts on File Inc., New York, 1978, p. 6
8 N.K. Denzin, 'Collective behaviour in total institutions: the case of the mental hospital and prison', *Sociological Problems*, 15 (3), 1968, pp. 353–65
9 V. Fox, 'Prison disciplinary problems', in J. Johnston et al. (eds.), *Society of Punishment and Corrections*, Wiley and Sons, New York, 1962, p. 396
10 E. Goffman and J. Garfinkely, 'Conditions of successful degradation ceremonies', *American Journal of Sociology*, 61 (5), 1956, pp. 402–25
11 A. Krista, *Deadlier than the Male: Violence and Aggression in Women*, Manpa Collins, London, 1994, p. 45
12 Colin Crawford, *Forbidden Femininity: Child Sexual Abuse and Female Sexuality*, Ashgate Press, Aldershot, 1998, pp. 32–3, 76
13. Clarence Schrag, 'Leadership among prison inmates' in J. Johnston et al. (eds.), *Society of Punishment and Corrections*, Wiley and Sons, New York, 1962, pp. 419–22
14 Lloyd McCorkle, 'Guard inmate relationships' in J. Johnston et al. (eds.), *Society of Punishment and Corrections*, Wiley and Sons, New York, 1962, pp. 429–34
15 Philip Zimbardo, 'The mind is a formidable jailer', *New York Times Magazine*, 8 April 1973
16 John Sabini, 'Aggression in the laboratory' in J.L. Kutash et al. (eds.), *Violence*, Josey Bass Inc., San Francisco, 1978, pp. 368–9
17 *Ibid*.
18 G.M. Sykes and M. Messenger, *The Inmate Social System: Theoretical Studies in the Social Organisation of the Prison*, Social Science Research Council, New York, 1960, pp. 8–9

Chapter 3

1 John Darby, *Conflict in Northern Ireland: The Development of a Polarised Community*, Gill and Macmillan, Dublin, 1976, p. 36
2 Paddy Hillyard, 'Law and order', in John Darby (ed.), *Northern Ireland: A Background to the Conflict*, Appletree Press/Syracuse University Press, Belfast and Syracuse, 1983, p. 36
3 Tim Pat Coogan, *On the Blanket: The H Block Story*, Ward River Press, Dublin, 1980, pp. 46–67
4 *Ibid*.
5 J. Bowyer Bell, *The Secret Army: A History of the IRA*, Academy Press, Dublin, 1979, pp. 388–91

6 Hillyard (1983), p. 37
7 Coogan (1980), pp. 46–67
8 Zimbardo (1973)
9 Interview with Gusty Spence, UVF OC, June 1979
10 D. Glasier, *The Effectiveness of a Prison and Parole System*, Bobbs, Merril, Indianapolis, 1964, p. 212

Chapter 4

1 Carl G. Jung, *Four Archetypes*, Routledge and Kegan Paul, London, 1972, pp. 16–17
2 Bill Rolston, 'Reformism and sectarianism: state of the Union after civil rights' in John Darby (ed.), *Northern Ireland: A Background to the Conflict*, Appletree Press/Syracuse University Press, Belfast and Syracuse, 1983, pp. 197–224
3 M. Poole, 'The demography of violence' in John Darby (ed.), *Northern Ireland: A Background to the Conflict*, Appletree Press/ Syracuse University Press, Belfast and Syracuse, 1983, pp. 151–80
4 Boulton (1973), pp. 40–1
5 Colin Crawford, 'In defence of status: prison strategies and the Northern Ireland conflict', unpublished M.Phil. thesis, University of Bradford, 1993, p. 82
6 *Ibid*, p. 96
7 Quoted in Boulding (1963), pp. 309–10
8 *Belfast Telegraph*, 9 September 1974
9 *Irish Press*, Dublin, 17 October 1974
10 *Irish News*, Belfast, 17 October 1974
11 *News Letter*, Belfast, 17 October 1974
12 *News Letter*, Belfast, 18 November 1978
13 *Irish News*, Belfast, 18 May 1977
14 *News Letter*, Belfast, 11 May 1977
15 S. Nelson, 'The Ulster independance debate', *Fortnight*, Belfast, 14 January 1977
16 Paul Bew and Gordon Gillespie, *Northern Ireland. A Chronology of the Troubles*, Gill and Macmillan, Dublin, 1993, p. 91
17 *Ibid.*, p. 99
18 *Ibid.*
19 *Ibid.*
20 *Ibid.*
21 Northern Ireland Office White Paper, Cmnd 5675, HMSO, Belfast, 1975

22 Bew and Gillespie (1993), p. 106
23 Bowyer Bell (1979), p. 398
24 *Ibid.*, p. 410

Chapter 5

1 Colin Crawford, 'Long Kesh: an alternative perspective', unpublished M.Sc. thesis, 1980, Cranfield Institute of Technology, Bedford
2 Interview with UDA prisoner, Long Kesh, 1979
3 In 1979 I identified and documented the advantages of the compound system and sent my findings to the Northern Ireland Office.
4 Edwin Sutherland, *The Professional Thief*, University of Chicago Press, Chicago, 1937, pp. 82–3
5 Coogan (1980), p. 80
6 Provisional IRA Standing Orders, 1976 – a Long Kesh document provided by David Morley
7 Interview with loyalist prisoner, June 1997
8 Statement by Bishop Cahal B. Daly, 1 January 1979, quoted in Coogan (1980), pp. 177–8
9 *Sunday News*, Belfast, 4 November 1979
10 Interestingly, some of the loyalist prisoners who had tobacco were obliged to use the only paper available to them to roll their cigarettes – pages of the Bible. One former loyalist prisoner remarked upon how 'an IRA killer' in the cell next to him refrained from doing this. 'He'd killed men, and yet he wouldn't tear a wee bit of paper out of the Bible to smoke.' Some loyalist and republican prisoners in conditions of abject deprivation had shared their pathetically small rations of tobacco, dangerously smuggled in.
11 Statement by Cardinal Tomas Ó Fiaich on 2 August 1978 after visiting protesting prisoners in the H-Blocks, quoted in Coogan (1980), pp. 158–60

Chapter 6

1 Interview with loyalist life sentence prisoner, July 1997
2 *Irish News*, Belfast, 13 May 1981
3 *Sunday Times*, London, 17 May 1981

4 *Ibid.*

5 *Ibid.*

6 *Sunday Independent*, Dublin, 24 May 1981

7 *Sunday Times,* London, 31 May 1981

8 *Daily Mirror*, London, 27 April 1981

9 *Observer*, London, 3 May 1981

10 Padraig O'Malley, *The Uncivil Wars: Ireland Today*, Blackstaff Press, Belfast, 1983, p. 254

11 *Sunday Press*, Dublin, 31 May 1981

12 O'Malley (1983), p. 3

13 *Sunday Times*, London, 12 April 1981

PART TWO

Introduction

The purpose of the first part of my research during the years 1986–90 was to examine the prisoners' day-to-day experience of imprisonment under both the compound regime and the H–Block regime. I carried out face-to-face interviews with eighty former prisoners, representing loyalists, republicans and 'ordinary' criminal offenders as follows:

UDA/UFF prisoners	30
UVF/RHC prisoners	30
PIRA prisoners	10
ordinary criminal prisoners	10

My intention had been to interview twenty-five men from each prisoner group, but I was unable to access a sufficient number from the last two groups.

The second part of the research was carried out during 1996–7 and involved in-depth, face-to-face interviews with fifty loyalist life sentence ex-prisoners drawn from the ranks of the UDA, UFF, UVF and RHC. The interviewing entailed sociological and psychological profiling of the men, their experience of imprisonment in the two regimes, and brief post-release histories.

I had not originally planned what became the third part of this research – prison officer experience of the compound and H–Block systems. I had discounted any possibility of securing access to prison officers, or, in the unlikely event of clearing that hurdle, of gaining their co-operation in research focusing on such a controversial issue. As things turned out, three ex-prison officers were interviewed in 1998, simply with a view to getting 'the other side of the story'. However, the corroborative nature of their testimonies, from so unexpected a source, is in itself a powerful indictment of the government's criminalisation policy.

Interviews with Ex-prisoners
1986–1990

Methodology

There was no scientific basis to the sampling. The rationale was to inter-view by semi-structured questionnaire as many ex-prisoners as possible within given time constraints. It would have been possible to interview more loyalist ex-prisoners but there was already so much duplication in the emerging themes that this was deemed unnecessary. This research is both qualitative and quantitative, and while the statistical analysis does provide for useful data, I was more concerned to present the human story behind the percentages and bar charts.

Presentation of Findings

For the purpose of presenting the research findings, the former prisoner groups are considered under the following categories and abbreviations:

loyalist ex-prisoner, Compound	LC
loyalist ex-prisoner, H–Block	LHB
republican ex-prisoner, Compound	RC
republican ex-prisoner, H–Block	RHB
ordinary decent criminal★	ODC

★'Ordinary decent criminal' was the official description for criminal offenders in Northern Ireland as from 1976, used to differentiate these offenders from the Special Category, or political, prisoners.

The first group of questions was designed to identify the various factors which led to a prisoner's offence and/or to his paramilitary involvement. Of the ordinary criminal offender group, 40 per cent identified 'psychological' or 'personality' factors as important in their offending. Forty per cent indicated that they had been motivated by a desire for 'amusement' and 70 per cent through 'personal gain'; 100 per cent replied that their involvement was criminal. This range of pre-disposing 'criminal' factors had no application in the replies of former paramilitary, or political, prisoners.

Environment and peer group relationships were seen as significant to all groups. However, one point of differentiation was membership of paramilitary or criminal cultures. Membership of a peer group was markedly less significant for former loyalist paramilitary prisoners, who were much more likely to act independently. Loyalists were also more likely to have considered themselves 'at war' and to regard their actions as reactive. Republicans placed a high importance on advancing their ideology or culture. One hundred per cent of all former paramilitary prisoners identified the motivation in their involvement as 'political'.

'Do you have a history of "getting into trouble" and would you be ordinarily inclined to break the law?'

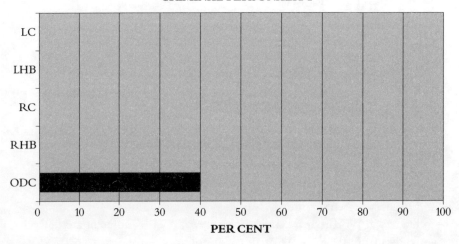

CRIMINAL PERSONALITY

'Do you feel that the environment you lived in was significant to your
paramilitary involvement or criminal offending?'

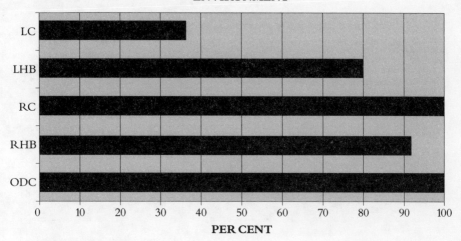

'Do you feel that the association with your friends, or peer group, was
significant to your paramilitary involvement or criminal offending?'

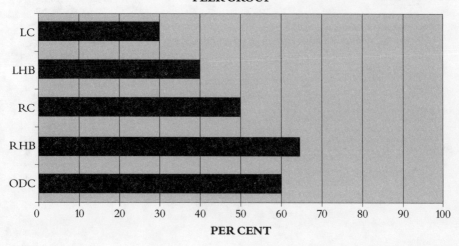

'Did you become involved in paramilitary activity/criminal offending because of a perception that (A) a state of war existed in Northern Ireland or (B) to advance a political ideology?'

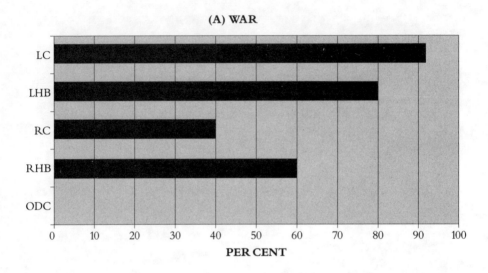

(A) WAR

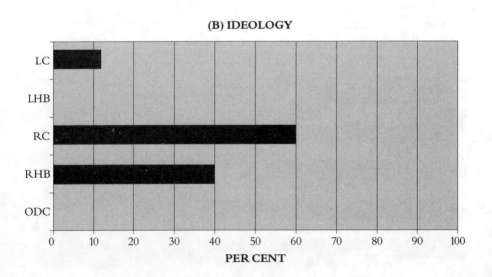

(B) IDEOLOGY

'Do you feel your paramilitary involvement/criminal offending was reactive and in response to attacks upon your community?'

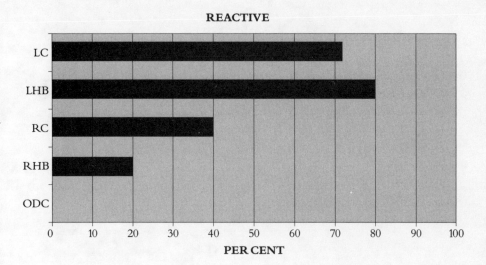

'Was your paramilitary involvement/criminal offending politically motivated?'

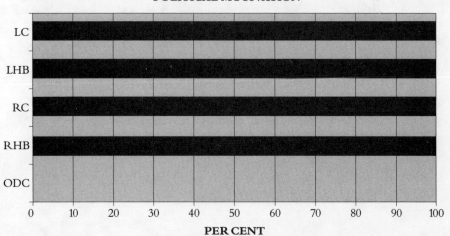

'Did you become involved in paramilitary activity/criminal offending for reasons of (A) amusement or (B) personal gain?'

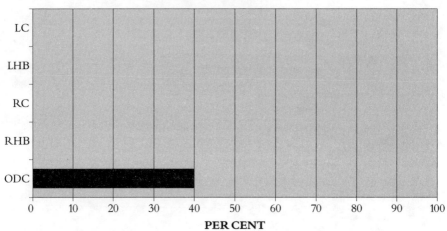

(A) AMUSEMENT

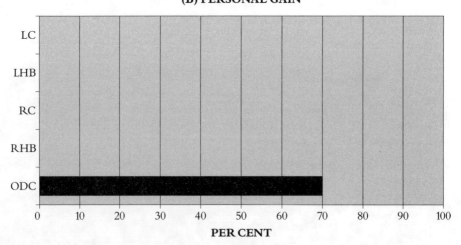

(B) PERSONAL GAIN

'Was your paramilitary involvement/criminal offending motivated through criminal intent?'

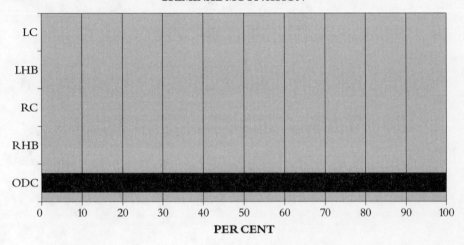

The second group of questions was designed to reveal prisoners' perceptions of the circumstances and the effect of their imprisonment.

'How would you describe the circumstances of your imprisonment? (A) humane containment, (B) rehabilitative or (C) punitive?'

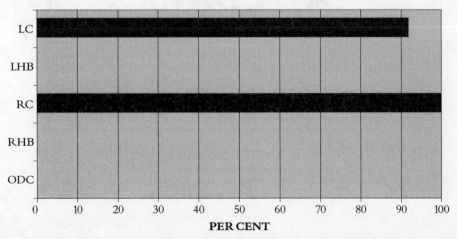

(B) REHABILITATIVE

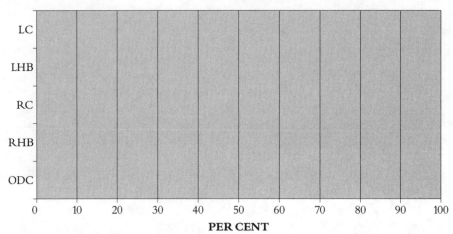

(C) PUNITIVE

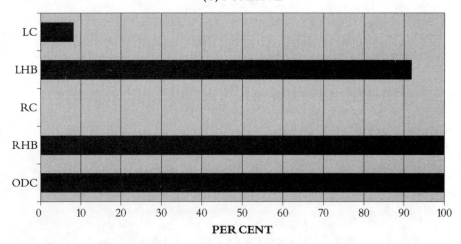

'Would your experience of imprisonment deter you from further paramilitary or criminal involvement?'

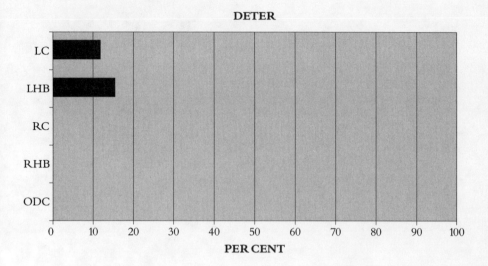

'Would your experience of imprisonment further incline you toward paramilitary or criminal involvement?'

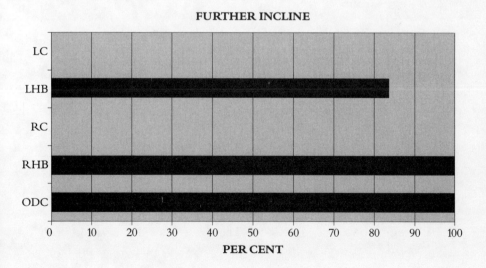

'Would your experience of imprisonment have no effect upon you?'

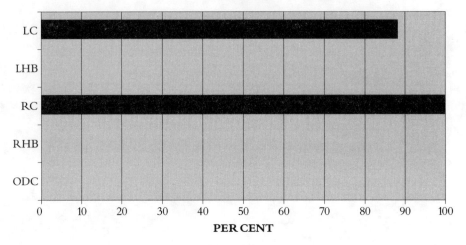

NO EFFECT

A representative selection of comments by former prisoners follows.

UDA/UFF Group

CIRCUMSTANCES OF IMPRISONMENT: COMPOUND PRISONERS

'It was humane containment, but there was punishment, the deprivation of liberty.'

'No time in prison is easy, but at least in the compounds you were treated like an individual, a person, unlike other prisons where you were an anonymous number.'

'Compared to the H-Blocks it was humane containment. The compounds were bad enough, God knows what it must be like in the blocks.'

'Humane containment probably covers it best from the list. Although I could think of ways in which it could have been more humane, particularly regarding access to family. They were doing a sentence as surely as I was.'

'Separation was painful, not imprisonment. Other prisoners could make your time hard.'

'The compound system did not involve humiliation or degradation . . . It allowed for a degree of respect between prisoners and staff.'

'I can only see it as punishment – they punish you by locking you up in a large cage with eighty other men, like an animal in a zoo – that's got to be punishment.'

'I did time in an ordinary system as well, and if anything it was easier to take. The day was structured for you . . . broken into segments and you were in different places. In the compounds it's the boredom, the sameness, everything within the cage.'

H-BLOCK PRISONERS

'There's no way you could link treatment or rehabilitation with what went on in the blocks. The screws were a shower of bastards who got the boot in at every chance.'

'Every day was a punishment, something to be endured and got through. The screws enjoyed putting you down.'

'H-Block was about pure punishment. They wanted to break you and make you accept a criminal status.'

'You were treated not like a normal person, but an animal, degraded.'

'I was very naïve before I went into prison. I thought that if you were decent to people they were decent back. Inside the screws were out to get you. They took a pleasure in putting you down; it made them feel big.'

EFFECTS OF IMPRISONMENT: COMPOUND PRISONERS

'Yes, it would deter me – I don't want to go back, but I have a loyalty to my people, and to the UDA.'

'Put it like this, I never want to go back. I honestly don't know if I could take it again. Prison affects different people differently – I found it very hard to do.'

'Nobody wants to be in prison . . . As a political offender I see the circumstances of imprisonment as largely irrelevant.'

'As a political offender it would neither deter me or make me more inclined toward further offending.'

'Re-involvement would depend on the level of conflict outside prison.'

H-BLOCK PRISONERS

'After you come out of prison you are very bitter. It's like a huge chip on your shoulder. You may be fairly normal when you go in but it's a long time before you're normal after you come out. It's the way you're treated by the screws; you're made to feel something less than human.'

'I felt and feel extremely aggressive towards prison officers – I'd go for them in the street. I got slapped about, and saw friends getting worked over. The injustice was hard to take. Call me "Sir", being treated like a dog – I wouldn't call my own father "Sir". I didn't return home for a long time. I lost my confidence and my self-respect. Treatment like that can only make you worse.'

'I wasn't really a hard man before I went in, but I was when I got out. I hadn't realised that I could hate as much as I hated the screws.'

'H-Block, in my opinion, made everyone worse. You got more bitter. One of my mates saw a screw in the street and went for him; he ended up doing time for it. He hated them so much he couldn't help it. We all hated the bastards.'

'They treated you like an animal, and sure enough in some ways that's what you became. One of the main things that keeps you going is hatred for screws.'

'After you come out you've got to forget what you have gone through – if you don't or can't, you've had it. I could so I was all right.'

UVF/RHC Group

CIRCUMSTANCES OF IMPRISONMENT: COMPOUND PRISONERS

'We were subject to the discipline of our own officers, and this was accepted. The situation required control and this was best handled by our own people. Screws could never have done that.'

'Found nothing wrong with the compound system whatsoever. It was a natural arrangement and the best arrangement.'

'Humane containment, although strict discipline was imposed by leaders in the compound – this was accepted as being in the interests of the total group.'

'Humane containment. There was very limited contact with screws or welfare staff – which suited the men.'

'Humane containment. It allowed you to keep your identity and sense of self-respect.'

H-BLOCK PRISONERS

'Punishment – anybody who could call that rehabilitation or treatment needs fucking certified.'

'The H-Blocks were all about punishment – trying to break men down mentally.'

'The blocks are just hell holes. Screws harassed and provoked men to try and break them down. The sick part was, they enjoyed it.'

'Punishment. You were treated like an animal. It was their whole attitude to you. Personal abuse, diggings, victimisation.'

EFFECTS OF IMPRISONMENT: COMPOUND PRISONERS

'In the compounds we were like an autonomous group. Self-sufficient. The screws left us alone. We did our thing and they did theirs.'

'Doing time in the compounds, generally speaking, wasn't a problem. Being separated from your family was the problem.'

'I suppose you could have called it humane containment. There was never any question of any prisoners being abused. We could have gone over the wire at any time and they knew that, so they left us alone.'

'It was easy time. I knew what was happening to the boys in the blocks and I felt guilty about that. We should have used our strength to improve their conditions.'

H-BLOCK PRISONERS

'It was a borstal system. Grown men, political prisoners, treated worse than animals. I never heard anything about rehabilitation or treatment. All I knew about was the mistreatment.'

'They were trying to criminalise us, turn us into fucking animals. We knew that we weren't and we fought them, but, Jesus, did we pay for it.'

'Ordinary decent fellas went into that system and they came out as psychopaths. You could see the hatred in their eyes; you could taste it. It was an evil regime.'

'What I couldn't understand was that the screws were Protestants who referred to themselves as "loyalists". I'd say, What's that [loyalist] tattoo on your arm? And they'd try to hide it. They weren't loyalists; those boys were scum.'

'You were never the same after it. Nobody understood what you'd been through. I was never the same with my wife and kids. The only person I can really talk to is ——, and that's because we went through it together.'

'When I first went into the blocks my number one first enemy was the IRA. It didn't take long to discover that the real enemy were the screws.'

PIRA Group

CIRCUMSTANCES OF IMPRISONMENT: COMPOUND PRISONERS

'If you had to call it one of those things, I suppose it would be humane containment. They left us alone to do our time. That's not to say anyone enjoyed it or found it easy, even if they say that. Being locked up is never easy.'

'We know we were well off in the compounds compared to the blocks.'

'Humane containment. It was imprisonment being locked up in cages, but compared to the blocks, it was no problem. We were under our own leadership and everyone accepted that. In fact our men did the screws' work for them, if you like. It only took a couple of screws to man the gate, and that was it.'

'It was humane containment. Institutional forces were at a minimum. You had free choice when to eat, who to talk to, what to do. You had fifty men to choose who to talk to. In the blocks you'd be locked up with one other man.'

H–BLOCK PRISONERS

'The screws treated us like dirt. They hated us and did everything they could to break our morale and spirit. It was our very hatred for the screws which kept our morale so good, in the circumstances.'

'Treatment and rehabilitation? That's a joke. We got treated badly in prison, but what else would you expect? Prison is part of the oppressive machinery of the state, they are out to break you.'

'There's no prison that can rehabilitate or treat you. You can't punish a man that way and expect him to get better; he'll only get worse.'

'The screws were out to get you all the time. The younger prisoners were scared stiff of them; you could see fear in their eyes. They enjoyed picking on them.'

EFFECTS OF IMPRISONMENT: COMPOUND PRISONERS

'I was in prison for political reasons. If I went back in it would be for political reasons. Prison wouldn't have anything to do with it.'

'The compounds had no real effect on me, it was a few years out of your life and that was that.'

'It's hard to say how it affected me. It made me very aware of all the things I was missing. My wife and family, going out for a drink. It made me appreciate what I had a lot more.'

'I came out more or less the same way I went in.'

H-BLOCK PRISONERS

'Prison and the way you're treated is part of the bigger problem. Anyone who went through it knew that they were right to fight against such a system – and what it represents.'

'In one respect imprisonment had a limited effect upon me. But it did make me feel more alientated. It reinforced the sense of injustice which led to my involvement in the first place.'

'Before I went into prison I may have had some reservations about everything we do. I learnt better – prison educates you in that way. There's only one reality, them and us, and the armed struggle.'

ODC Group

The 'criminal' group had no access to the 'political' compounds, and consequently they were all imprisoned in the H-Blocks.

CIRCUMSTANCES OF IMPRISONMENT

'Pure punishment – rehabilitation and treatment were things I never heard about, and never saw in prison. Just men being made to do hard time.'

'Learned me a bit about crime and not getting caught. Made me bitter against police, courts, especially screws, and the whole fucking system.'

'Jesus, prison didn't do much for me. It only teaches one thing, you're on one side and they're on the other. Anything goes.'

'The screws treated you like an animal. They weren't interested in humane treatment or rehabilitation, they were out to degrade and punish – that made them feel good.'

'Humane containment? That's a joke. It was punishment from the minute you went in until the minute you went out. Do this, do that, say "Sir" – made to feel like a wee boy all the time.'

EFFECTS OF IMPRISONMENT

'I think, if anything, it would make you inclined to get into further trouble. I saw men in for petty things come out like gangsters. Fellas who were dead nice, easy going, turn into "hards". It does that all right.'

'Nobody wants to be back into prison. If anything, it made you worse – more bitter, more hostile. There was no justice in there, the screws lied in front of the governor to get you into trouble. I fucking hated them; they bust the rules inside and expected you to play by the rules outside.'

'Made me more bitter against prison system, police, prison officers, courts, society in general. It would . . . make you want or even need to get back at them.'

'The treatment, if you could call it that, was brutal, they got at you mentally all the time, rubbing your nose in the shit. That made them big men.'

'I was a fucking nervous wreck in there. My nerves aren't better yet. I was never like that before I went in.'

'If they think it does anybody any good, they ought to try it. It wouldn't put me off, it would make me bloody worse. I get angry just talking about it.'

'You're never the same after you come out, you know they've done their worst, and that you could take it. You lose your self-respect and nothing you do matters after that.'

The third and fourth groups of questions tested the perceived levels of personal and interpersonal strain and revenge motivation experienced as a consequence of imprisonment.

'Did the experience of imprisonment place a psychological strain upon . . .?'

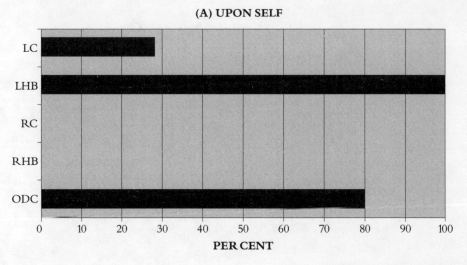

(A) UPON SELF

(B) UPON FAMILY

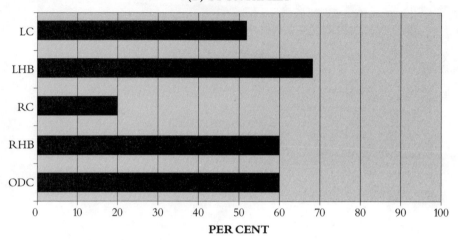

(C) UPON PEER RELATIONSHIPS

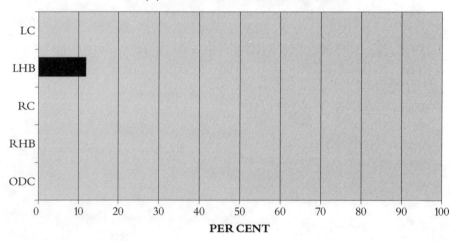

(D) WITH STATE AUTHORITY

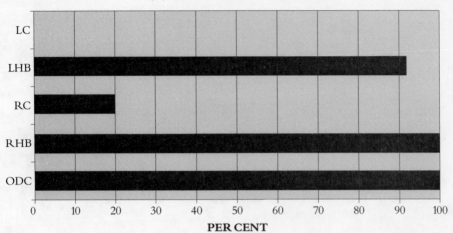

PER CENT

(E) WITH AUTHORITY IN GENERAL

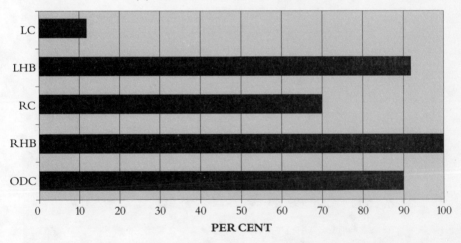

PER CENT

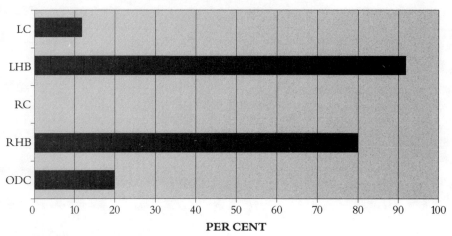

'As a direct result of your imprisonment did you experience a need to "get back" at authority or society in general?'

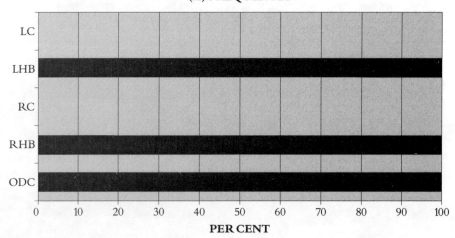

(B) INFREQUENTLY

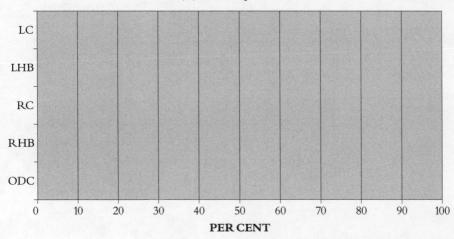

PER CENT

(C) NEVER

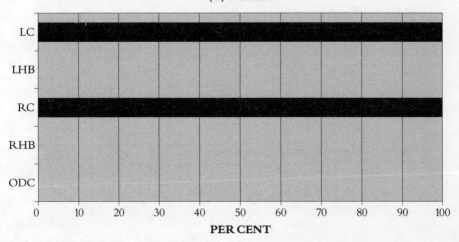

PER CENT

A representative selection of comments by former prisoners follows.

UDA/UFF Group

STRAIN FACTOR: COMPOUND PRISONERS

'The strain factor was minimal. My personal friendship network was unaffected, probably due to the political nature of the offence, and the fact that my family and friends accepted that. I didn't have any bad feelings toward the prison officers, police, or security forces – the reality was I was doing their job.'

'Being inside nearly wrecked my parents. They didn't understand what was happening – we'd be in a united Ireland before they understood.'

'I was engaged and it was a strain. Had it been a self-gain offence, the wedding would have been off.'

H-BLOCK PRISONERS

'The state, authority, whatever, they treated you the way they did, like you were a dog. Of course you resent it and become bitter.'

'I have never felt the same since prison – it's like I always feel dirty. I was stupid before I went in. I thought we always played by the rules – I'd no idea what went on inside. When screws were shot by the IRA I was glad, for once maybe I agreed with what they were doing.'

'They [prison officers] tried to crack you up . . . If you gave in to them, you'd had it.'

'You always felt dirty in prison. Treated like a wee boy, calling screws "Sir" when they were just dirt. Having to wear a prison uniform somehow reduced you as a person – you were not a man so much as a number.'

REVENGE MOTIVATION: COMPOUND PRISONERS

'There was nobody to get back at except the IRA. We were in there because of the IRA.'

A prisoner who had experienced both compound and H-Block systems responded: 'In the compounds they did not have access to you to degrade you or dehumanise you. The major problem in prison [the H–Blocks] was the attitude of prison staff, the physical conditions, the uniform – the fact that they never fitted and you felt like a prick, shoes two sizes too big, pants too big, et cetera. In the compounds you didn't have those problems, you still had to do time, and any time is hard, but you didn't have all that shit. The fact that we were allowed to be human, meant the screws could be human – it's hard to explain.'

'We had very limited contact with the screws – they were usually friendly enough. It could be a very lonely job for them.'

'The screws were decent enough with us, so we'd nothing against them.'

'In the compound the screws treated us OK, and we treated them the same way. I hadn't much to do with the screws in the compound, but any time we met them they were OK.'

H-BLOCK PRISONERS

'I hated them [prison officers], and they hated me. Nothing would have given me greater satisfaction than going for one of them man to man, but they are not "man" enough for that. You went for one of them, you got thrown onto the boards [punishment cells] and six of them saw to you.'

'You always wanted to get back at the screws. Just thinking about that kept you going, only somehow you never did it when you got out. It was the thought of doing time again for one of those bastards . . .'

'I always wanted to get back at the screws – not the police or anyone else, they were just doing their job. But the screws were different – those guys were fucking dirt.'

UVF/RHC Group

STRAIN FACTOR: COMPOUND PRISONERS

'I found paramilitary discipline hard to take, but you could opt out. At least you could reason with your own people, unlike the screws.'

'It was hard to get your time in – in the compounds there was no structure to the day. The paramilitary leadership tried to organise things but there was resistance.'

'I felt being inside was unfair – what I did was for my country.'

H–BLOCK PRISONERS

'If it were not for the organisation and back-up of the paramilitaries, loyalist prisoners would have been fair game in the blocks. We were badly outnumbered, and if you weren't connected [affiliated to a paramilitary group] you were in trouble.'

'I got stronger tied to the organisation in the blocks to fight the republicans and the system. The prison officers made new rules every day; you never knew what the rules were. You just stand there with your mouth shut and you lost twenty-one days' privileges.'

'If it weren't for the loyalist paramilitaries – UVF, UDA, RHC – we would have been wiped out. When organised we could protect ourselves. They knew anything they did to us inside might lead to action by the organisations outside.'

'It made me more dependent upon the paramilitary groups – they stood behind us and they were the only ones. We needed them for survival.'

'My nerves have been shot ever since I came out. I blow up at the least thing.'

REVENGE MOTIVATION: COMPOUND PRISONERS

'The security forces did their job, just like the screws, there was no hard feeling.'

'We just didn't think like that [about revenge]. There was never any reason to.'

'The compounds just weren't like that.'

'The screws were all right with us, and we left them alone to get on with their job, which was security after all.'

H–BLOCK PRISONERS

'Yes, I frequently wanted to get revenge. I wanted to get back at them [prison officers] outside prison. Physically, and seriously.'

'Thinking about getting back at the screws, and the Provos, kept you going.'

'Most of the screws were animals, but there was the odd decent one. I wouldn't have mined touching for some of those fucking bastards.'

'Prison officers in particular. I felt a real need to get back physically.'

'Definitely. I saw a screw in a loyalist club and I was going to touch for him, but he got offside quick.'

'I never talk about screws because it makes me fucking crazy. A lot of things will be settled before this is over.'

PIRA Group

STRAIN FACTOR: COMPOUND PRISONERS

'I didn't experience any strain because of actual imprisonment. My attitudes towards the British are exactly the same now as they were before I went in.'

'I didn't feel any strain because of imprisonent. I am a republican, and therefore any strain I felt in relation to the British was already there.'

'You had a choice of whether to stay in the compound or not. The alternative being the H–Blocks. Only two republicans ever left of their choice that I knew of.'

'I can't say I found any strain in my relationship because of being inside. Some guys found it hard to take, but to me it was OK. Everybody understood why I was in'.

H-BLOCK PRISONERS

'It was us and them, there were no shades of grey. When you went in there you knew you were at war. They tried to turn you into a criminal but that only made you more conscious of what you were, a political prisoner. If it were any different they wouldn't have had to try so hard.'

'Yes, it made me hate prison officers. But I already felt a strain in my relationship with state authority – we always hated the police – RUC, army, whatever.'

'If it hadn't been for the organisation and the other men, it would have been hell. They, the screws, were out to break you and they did not hide the fact. The more they tried to criminalise us, the greater was our sense of solidarity and identity as political prisoners.'

'It made you very dependent on your paramilitary group. You were threatened by the loyalists, mixing with criminal offenders – which made you realise how different you were from them, and reinforced your sense of being a political offender, and the screws were trying to get at you all the time, to make *you* feel like a criminal!'

REVENGE MOTIVATION: COMPOUND PRISONERS

'Never. The screws were fairly decent with us, and we didn't bother them. They did their own thing and we did ours.'

'I never thought about it like that, but I see what you are getting at – it might have been different if I'd been in the blocks.'

'Never. We got on reasonably well with the screws.'

'Never. The screws were OK with us. You just would never have thought like that – except we knew what was going on in the blocks.'

H-BLOCK PRISONERS

'I hated the screws. It's hatred which keeps you going. If they had been nice to us – and there's no way they could have been – we wouldn't have known what to do with ourselves. Obviously we wanted to get back at them, and we did; only, when we got one of them outside, we paid for it inside.'

'We knew what the screws had done to the boys to break the dirty protest. Of course we wanted to get back at them. They were part of the British war machine – legitimate targets.'

'You hated the screws all right, but you just did your time, as there was nothing you could do until you got out.'

'We hated them and they hated us. Yes, we were highly revenge motivated but we had to follow the organisation's policy, which played down confrontation.'

ODC Group

STRAIN FACTOR

'Prison officers were a shower of bastards. You had to fight them all the time, otherwise you became an animal and that's what they wanted.

When you heard of one getting shot you were glad.'

'There were times inside when I felt like killing myself just to end it all. Some people tried that. But you can't let them [prison officers] win. How the hell can you have any respect for authority after that; the authorities look after themselves regardless of the cost to anyone else.'

'The H-Blocks were hell holes; for a long time you were lost, then you got depressed, then you got angry. I've been angry ever since.'

'It's hard to explain, but it really fucks you up. You're made to feel like a wee boy. You want to go for them but you can't. Then you hate yourself for not doing it. They've got you and that's that.'

'Sometimes I thought I was going to crack up. Plenty of fellas did that, swallowed razor blades and all that. That's what the system and the screws want. After they break you they can do what they want, and you become a sign of their power to frighten others.'

REVENGE MOTIVATION

'You might think about it but where would that get you? You'd end up in prison for the rest of your life.'

'You'll probably laugh, but I used to dream about shooting police officers, screws . . . What right does he have for God-like power? When I get drunk I want to take on the police. I don't think prison does anybody any good; it makes you hate the system and yourself.'

'I wanted to go for screws all the time, but you knew they'd kick your shit in for doing that. We saw it happen to some of the lads. They push you on purpose so you will go for them, then a group of them touch for you. Big men. There's a word for people like that – sadists. They say it's in all of us – it's in them all right, it's how they get their excitement.'

The fifth and sixth groups of questions were designed to ascertain a record of disciplinary proceedings against the former prisoners and to discern their views on the effectiveness of different penal systems in preventing further crime.

'Were you subject to disciplinary proceedings during your imprisonment?'

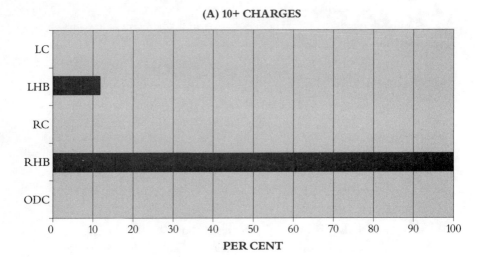

(A) 10+ CHARGES

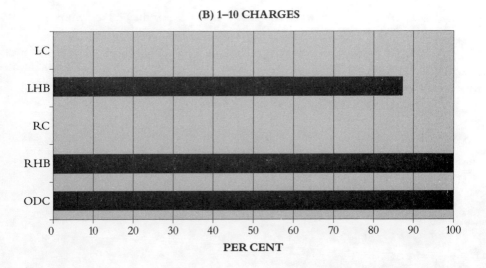

(B) 1–10 CHARGES

(C) NO CHARGES

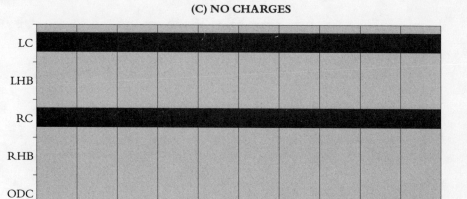

'Which conditions of imprisonment, in your view, help prevent further crime?'

(D) HUMANE CONTAINMENT★

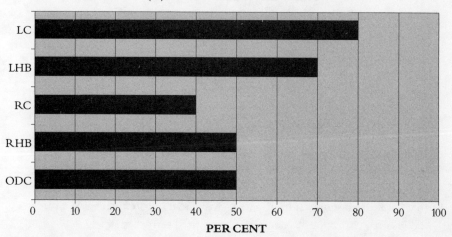

CONDITIONS IRRELEVANT

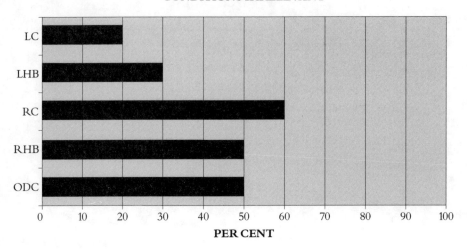

PER CENT

*None of the groups selected any of the other four options: (A) punitive penal regimes, (B) treatment orientated regimes, (C) rehabilitative regimes, or (E) other. It was felt that only humane containment helped prevent further crime or that the question was wholly irrelevant with regard to political offenders.

A representative selection of comments by former prisoners follows.

UDA/UFF Group

DISCIPLINARY PROCEEDINGS: COMPOUND PRISONERS

'Standards of discipline in the compounds were extremely high – we were under the control of our own officers and we accepted this authority in keeping order. We would never have accepted that from screws. In that sense the system ran itself – there were never more than two or three screws on a compound guarding one hundred terrorists.'

'Our own officers kept the men in line.'

'I often felt like hitting a screw [because of what was happening in the H-Blocks] but didn't. Not because of prison punishment, but because it was against organisation policy.'

'With political crime it doesn't matter what the prisons are like.'

H-BLOCK PRISONERS

'I was up on charges about six times. It's not what you did, more it was the way the screws showed their power over you. The fact that they could put you on a charge for nothing made you feel helpless, and them powerful. That's why it happened so often.'

'You wise up after a while – it's their fucking system and you can't beat them.'

'I was up on charges about five times – all for fucking stupid things, like not calling a screw "Sir". '

'All the charges I was up on were daft. If they didn't like the way you looked, they put you on a charge.'

MOST FUNCTIONAL PRISON SYSTEM: COMPOUND PRISONERS

'The compound system, because it's more humane. That's not to say it was easy. Nobody who's done time thinks it's easy, despite what they may say.'

'The really hard part of any sentence is being apart from your wife and family – losing your job, not having a social life. You take what you get when you go inside. You don't think about getting caught, never mind the conditions, when you're on the outside. The compounds are a better system than the blocks, but some fellas I know, who have done both, reckon time is longer in the cages [compounds] because, compared to the blocks, there's no action, nothing to get you worked up.'

'At the end of the day, prison conditions are probably irrelevant to the political offender.'

'It all depends upon political factors.'

'Men coming out of the compounds are usually quite normal. That's not the case in the blocks, whatever that sort of "treatment" does to men.'

H-BLOCK PRISONERS

'Humane containment, like the compounds. There was no aggro with the screws there, and the organisations [loyalist and republican] got on better as well. The compounds didn't screw men up like the blocks.'

'In the blocks they make criminals, that's what the "treatment" does.

They fuck you about so much, and for so long, you want to fuck somebody else up – almost to get it out of your system.'

'You can be an individual in the compounds and keep a sense of self-respect. There's no way you can do that in the blocks.'

'In the blocks rehabilitation means further punishment.'

'Treatment and rehabilitation in prison is a joke. Punishment like in the blocks only makes men more hard, more bitter, and more dangerous. I've seen it happen to friends of mine, who should never have been inside.'

UVF/RHC Group

DISCIPLINARY PROCEEDINGS: COMPOUND PRISONERS

'The compound system was a good system. It worked well for everyone. Some of the screws brought over from Scotland couldn't believe how relaxed it was.'

'We had our command structure and they had theirs. Any problems were sorted out between the OC and the assistant governor. It worked fine.'

'The first time I saw it I thought, Jesus, it's like a zoo. Men living in cages. But when you got in among your own it was fine. I actually still miss the crack.'

H-BLOCK PRISONERS

'I lost count of how many times I was up on charges. They knew I was the UVF OC of the wing, so I was a prime target for them. They thought if they broke me, the line of command would fall. I got it really rough.'

'They used to pick on the wee lads. Make them stand to attention; slap them around. I was going to go for them a couple of times, but you'd just get the fuck kicked out of you. You couldn't win.'

'The screws were a corrupt shower of bastards. They got the boot in at every chance.'

'There was bad treatment – they went too far. This was no ordinary prison regime. There were no prison rules as far as they were concerned. They were beyond the law, beyond control.'

MOST FUNCTIONAL PRISON SYSTEM: COMPOUND PRISONERS

'Prison is prison, no matter how you wrap it up. Nobody in his right mind would want to be in any prison, anywhere.'

'The conditions of imprisonment are irrelevant, before it happens. Obviously it makes a difference afterwards.'

'Putting a man in prison, any prison, does nothing to prevent further crime.'

'Personally, I think the conditions of imprisonment are irrelevant. Getting caught is the last thing you can afford to think about. It's dangerous riding a motorbike – if you thought you were going to get mangled every time you got on one, you wouldn't.'

H–BLOCK PRISONERS

'Punishment, as it is in the H–Blocks, can only make people worse. How could it do any good?'

'No contact with prison staff is the best arrangement. They are the problem in prison. They do the damage to people.'

'As a political offender, the conditions of imprisonment are irrelevant.'

'If everyone were equal and had the same, that would prevent "criminal crime". Peace would stop political offences, as far as the UVF is concerned.'

'Conditions of imprisonment are irrelevant – the height of the Troubles is the more important thing.'

PIRA Group

DISCIPLINARY PROCEEDINGS: COMPOUND PRISONERS

'None – we had very little to do with the screws.'

'We took care of our own discipline. We had our own rules and we stuck to them.'

'Never. Our own officers made sure that there was no trouble.'

H–BLOCK PRISONERS

'All I had to do was look at a screw and I got charged. I don't think they liked me.'

'We were put on the boards regularly. That's when the screws really got at you. They would beat the shit out of you.'

'You were put on the boards, for nothing, on a regular basis. It was all part of the policy to break us down, getting at us individually to break morale.'

MOST FUNCTIONAL PRISON SYSTEM: COMPOUND PRISONERS

'There's a big difference between criminal crime and armed resistance. The type of prison doesn't count when the man is politically motivated. Look what's happening recently. People are shot dead by the police because they are known to be involved – they can't get the evidence, so they shoot them.'

'I would say the compounds are better than the blocks.'

'I wouldn't like to have gone to the blocks, but it would not deter me. Guys risk getting shot dead. What the hell is a few years in prison compared to that?'

'If you have punishment on top of imprisonment, you can only make men more bitter, more resentful.'

H–BLOCK PRISONERS

'Probably humane containment, although the type of imprisonment is not a big thing. If you're going out on active service, you realise that you can get shut up, or shot dead.'

'The type of prison doesn't matter to politicals. The worse the conditions are in society, or in prison, the more we have a duty to struggle, resist, change. In that way, the more brutal the person, the more it strengthens our resolve and commitment, because when you're outside, you always know that people are paying the price inside.'

'Prison is a fact of life for an active republican, it always has been. When you get involved you don't even think about it, it goes without saying.'

'The type of prison doesn't matter when you are a political, but there's no doubt that H–Block can make you worse. I've seen that in a lot of my friends.'

ODC Group

DISCIPLINARY PROCEEDINGS

'They [prison officers] told lies on you to get you into trouble. Nobody gets into trouble on purpose because you know what would happen.'

'Nearly everybody does some time on the boards. It was all part of the package.'

'The screws tell you to watch yourself or you'll be on a charge. After that, you don't have to do anything, they think something up and charge you with it. Who's going to believe your word against them? They run the fucking place.'

MOST FUNCTIONAL PRISON SYSTEM

'Humane containment – just left alone to do your bird.'

'Ordinary imprisonment makes you worse. Maybe if you were treated decently, it wouldn't make you so bad. If you're treated like an animal, the chances are you become one. I seen it happen often enough.'

'Prison can't make people better, even the government knows that.'

'Humane containment would have to be better. Punishment, getting treated like an animal, what fucking good is that going to do anybody? You see it all the time, the more they do to you, pick on you, the worse you get, the more stick you get, on and on. Some of the fellas were never off the boards.'

'Humane containment. Punishment only makes people worse. I've seen people crack up in there, going out of the place mad, looking for trouble, back in within a week. Getting treated worse, and getting worse all the time.'

The seventh group of questions asked the former prisoners how they would describe the quality of their relationships with the prison staff.

'How would you describe the quality of your relationships (or interaction) with prison staff?'

(A) EXTREMELY BAD

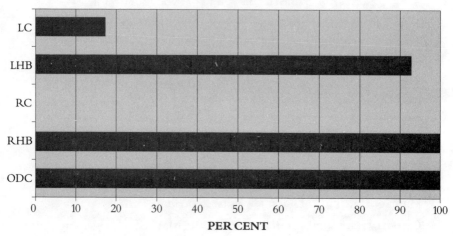

PER CENT

(B) BAD

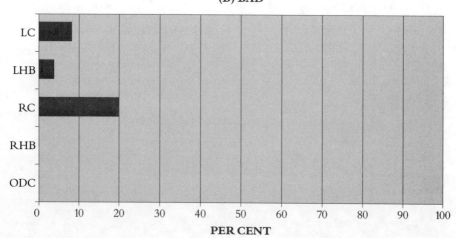

PER CENT

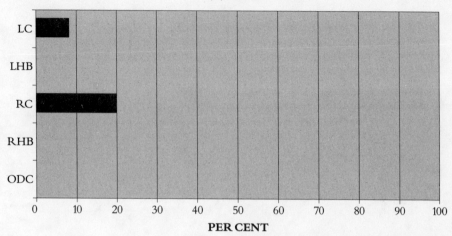

(C) GOOD

PER CENT

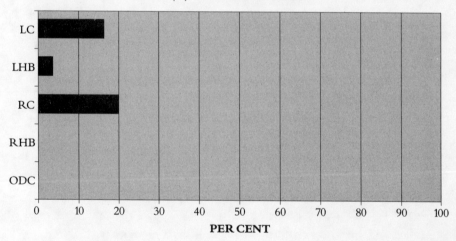

(D) EXTREMELY GOOD

PER CENT

(E) VERY LIMITED CONTACT

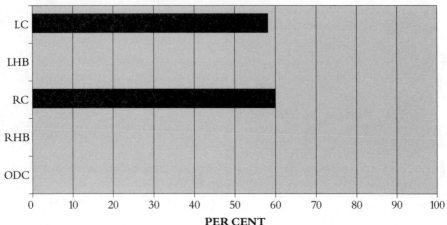

A representative selection of comments by former prisoners follows.

UDA/UFF Group

COMPOUND PRISONERS

'Prison staff were quite decent. One officer I know from Barlinnie [a high-security Scottish prison where the interviewee had served a sentence] described the compounds as a "gift". Prison officers in Barlinnie were, in effect, doing time along with you. The conditions in the compounds were comparatively excellent. I mean both for staff and prisoners.'

'Like I said, the screws were no problem – but sometimes we had to do their dirty work. If someone was going wire crazy and was going to go for one of them [prison officers], we watched him to make sure it didn't happen. I don't think that was our job – it was their prison, and their wire.'

'We had no problems with the screws and because of that, they had no problems from us.'

'I had very little contact with screws, there was no effect.'

H-BLOCK PRISONERS

'Relationships with prison staff made me very bitter. Showed me how corrupt ordinary people could become. That was the thing, they were nearly all Prods and from our districts. It's funny how they got like that.'

'Prison staff determined the quality of life, and that was bad.'

'Like I said, they treated you like an animal, what sort of a relationship could you have with them? They've no friends only themselves, who else would take them on?'

'It's funny, but you hate them so much it keeps you going – even wee things to annoy them can keep your spirits up for days.'

'They treated us like animals, but they were the real animals.'

UVF/RHC Group

COMPOUND PRISONERS

'We had very limited contact [with prison staff], which was good.'

'Never had any bother with screws.'

'We hadn't much to do with screws, apart from escort and lock up, and of course searches.'

'We were never mistreated by any of them and we didn't give them any trouble. The compounds were easier for prison officers – OCs [paramilitary compound leaders] could represent the prisoners and shortcut them having to see all the men.'

'We had no bother with screws – they were usually decent enough. We weren't encouraged to have relationships with them, and I think it was the same on their side.'

H-BLOCK PRISONERS

'Relationships with prison staff, if you could call them that, couldn't have been worse. They were only in it for the big salary – that's all. They didn't want to be there and they let you know all about it.'

'We hated them and they hated us, and that got worse and worse.'

'I was in both [systems] and it's hard to explain the difference – in the compounds the screws were normal – themselves – in the blocks they had to impress each other and senior staff about how hard they were, but with prisoners who couldn't fight back.'

'They were fucking bastards; they push you every way they can because they enjoy it.'

'Like I said, relationships with screws couldn't have been much worse.'

PIRA Group

COMPOUND PRISONERS

'There was never any bother, but we really didn't have much to do with them [prison officers]. Had no effect.'

'There was no bad feeling toward the screws – they didn't want our aggro and we didn't want theirs.'

'Very little to do with the screws – never had any bother with them.'

'We had very limited contact with the screws. Any necessary contact or negotiations would have been through the OC.'

H-BLOCK PRISONERS

'Relationships with prison staff really couldn't have been much worse. It was mutual hatred.'

'The screws were just dirt. Sometimes you wondered where the hell they could dig up so many.'

'Brutal, that's the only word for it.'

'Really bad. I honestly used to go to sleep and dream about meeting one on the outside, on his own, and breaking his fucking neck.'

ODC Group

'The screws were just dirt. The new ones coming in were OK for a while, then they got as bad.'

'Are you joking? Those fellas were the greatest pack of bastards on God's earth.'

'They were always on your back – you could never get away from them. Prison, and the way they treated me, made me fucking hate them.'

'Extremely bad. A relationship of mutual hatred. I learned to hate them [prison officers], the system, authorities in general.'

'Extremely bad – we hate the screws and they hate us.'

Discussion

The experience of imprisonment profiles are entirely consistent with the theoretical material presented in chapter 2. The emerging themes from those who experienced criminalisation in the H–Blocks were of hatred, bitterness, dehumanisation, abuse, abasement, degradation, and identity transformation. All these themes were considered theoretically and are here demonstrated to have a precise application in terms of those former prisoners subjected to criminalisation. Conversely, the compound system did provide for a system of humane containment, with virtually none of these negative psychological and sociological consequences. Accordingly, from any psychological, sociological, conflict resolution, or criminological perspective, the compound system should have been retained as a containment strategy for political prisoners.

These themes will be further examined, upon the basis of profiles of former loyalist life–sentence prisoners.

Interviews with Loyalist Ex-life-sentence Prisoners 1996–1997

It is interesting to note that I felt I had been involved in 'in-depth' interviews in my research presented in the previous chapter. In reality, however, while very significant themes were emerging, my research up to that point had only scratched the surface. I had accepted statements such as 'they [prison officers] couldn't have been worse' ... 'they were bastards' ... 'it was a hell hole', and so on, without asking the obvious follow-up questions – 'What exactly do you mean by that?' ... 'Describe that for me.' ... 'What actually happened?' ... This was rectified in the following research, with disturbing results.

There was no scientific basis to the sampling. All the life sentence ex-prisoners contacted who indicated a willingness to be interviewed were interviewed. Understandably many former life sentence prisoners did not wish to be reminded of their imprisonment, and others wished to maintain a distance from their past history. The contacts were made and interview arrangements established largely with the help of the Progressive Unionist Party, Ulster Democratic Party, the Ex-Prisoners' Interpretative Centre and the Post Conflict Resettlement Group.

The research which is both quantitative and qualitative is, once again, more concerned with the human story of fifty men and their families, caught up in the circumstance of conflict and war. The study fell into four parts, with questionnaires designed to probe the prisoner's sociological profile, psychological profile, his experience of imprisonment and his re-integration into society.

Sociological Profile

'How would you describe your home environment at the time of your arrest?'

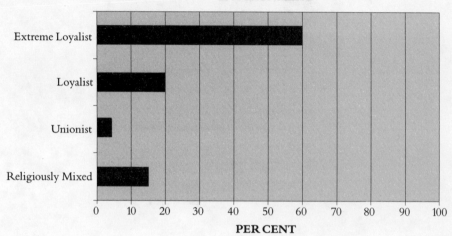

'How would you describe the economic conditions of the area in which you lived at the time of your arrest?'

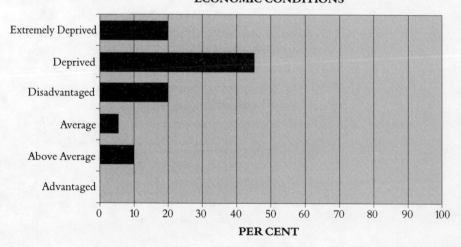

'How would you describe the class composition of the area in which you lived at the time of your arrest?'

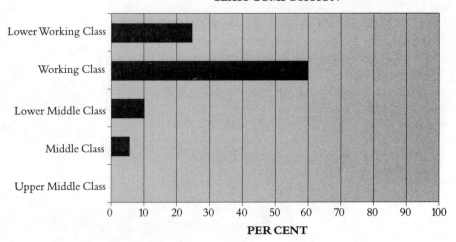

Eighty-five per cent of the group reported the class composition of their home environment as 'working class' or 'lower working class'. Some of the respondents reported experiencing extreme deprivation in their childhood, with household items being pawned on a weekly basis, memories of going hungry, fathers being unemployed and desperately seeking work. For some, fish and chips on a Friday night was the gastronomic event of the week – when they got it. Others told of their family's resistance to accepting National Assistance, because of a reluctance to 'accept charity' and fear of the stigma attached to receiving state benefits, which was seen as 'putting a strain on the British Exchequer'. A majority of the men, however, reported experiencing less deprived family circumstances: 'We may not have had much, but at least we were Protestant.' Fifteen per cent of the group reported lower-middle-class, or middle-class, home environments – all were rural and described themselves as 'countrymen'.

'Was the area in which you lived characterised by a high level of criminal activity at the time of your arrest?'

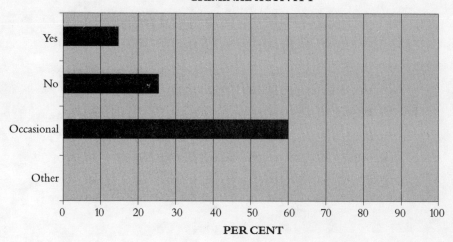

Fifteen per cent of the group reported a high level of criminal activity in their home environments at the time of their arrest – perhaps reflecting a breakdown of law and order which was a consequence of the conflict. By the late 1970s and the 1980s many areas in Northern Ireland were no longer policed in any conventional sense. In discussing criminal activity it is important to bear in mind that most of the group were sentenced to life imprisonment in the 1970s. At that time Northern Ireland had the lowest 'ordinary' crime rates in the United Kingdom. The 15 per cent reporting a high level of criminal activity in their home area tended to be those who were arrested in the 1980s. The rest of the group reported home environments which were characterised by occasional or little crime. It was generally reported that in loyalist areas at that time there was a strong stigma attached to criminal activity: 'You would look at someone who had committed a crime. They would be ostracised. Nobody would have trusted them or given them employment. People would talk about them . . . To commit a crime in those days was a terrible thing.'

'Was there a high level of loyalist paramilitary membership in your home area at the time of your arrest?'

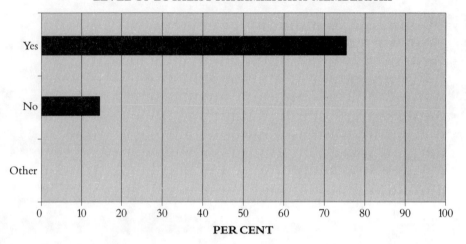

LEVEL OF LOYALIST PARAMILITARY MEMBERSHIP

In discussing the level of paramilitary activity in the group's 'home area' it became apparent that a dichotomy existed between urban and rural districts. In the loyalist 'ghetto' areas of Belfast a high level of paramilitary membership was reported:

'Where I lived nearly all the men were involved.'

'Paramilitary membership was more the norm than the exception.'

'The dogs in the street would give you the "nod".'

'It was a generational thing – the older generation didn't want to know, but we were all involved.'

'Very high. By the age of thirteen/fourteen I had developed an extreme hatred for Catholics, and it was mutual. There was sectarian street fights nearly every night, and that was before the guns came out. I had a six-foot portrait of King Billy in the house. My identity was extreme loyalist. When my son was born, I took a portrait of King Billy to the hospital for my wife. I pointed to the painting, then to my son, my wife and then myself – that's who he is, that's who you are, and that's who I am. Loyalists, loyalists to the end. Proud to live and proud to die . . .'

'Nearly everyone was a member of the paramilitaries, either UDA or UVF. However, there were a limited number of activists. They [the leaderships] had plenty of men to call on. If they had called on all of us, that would have been it – war . . .'

'Our area was under very heavy attack. We were surrounded by republican areas. The police and army were never there when they were needed. We'd be shot at nearly every night. It was a quasi-war situation. We had vigilantes, ex-services personnel, food houses, patrols. It was so bad, and we were so poorly armed, one of the men was caught trying to bring a gun back from England through the airport. He knew it was high risk, but that's how desperate we were . . .'

'There were more male residents in the area involved than not involved. Paramilitary membership was the norm.'

'In the past, yes, at times of trouble there were people you could call upon. Ninety-five per cent could be gathered for defensive purposes.'

'A majority of the men and women would have been involved. My mother was an extreme loyalist. She got me and my brother to volunteer. We would have done it anyway, but she couldn't wait. She used to sing "We fight for no surrender" doing the cleaning.'

Rural areas tended to be very different:

'The Protestant people tended to put their faith in the police and the UDR. In the country areas most families have people in the police and the UDR, so I suppose it was to be expected. Also in the country ordinary Protestants and Catholics have more respect for each other. I became involved almost by chance. When my wife and I got married we had to decide between a house in Bangor or in a town in mid-Ulster. We chose the town. There was a lot of trouble, police and UDR getting shot, the town was being bombed to hell. I was approached and I joined. I was middle class and I suppose I felt guilty that it was only working-class men doing all the fighting. I became very active, a so-called travelling gunman . . . That was it – choosing a house sealed my fate. I lost a secure, well-paid job, was separated from my wife and children for fifteen years. Seeing them suffer nearly killed me. I try to make it up to them, but I can't. Look at me now. The colleagues I worked with are nearly all retired, on fat pensions, and I'm doing this, just to scrape through.'

'I was a countryman. I suppose I wouldn't have become involved but for a close friend of mine being killed. He had been in the police. It wasn't a clean kill. He suffered horrendously. I was in the hospital with him and he was semi-conscious. I said, "——, I'm going to get the bastards who did this to you." I swear he smiled. I went to a loyalist bar in the town, and said, "Right, who the fuck is in charge here?" A big fella tapped the table with his glass and nodded over. That was it, I was in.'

'In the rural areas, membership was frowned upon. Loyalists were just like republicans. There were republican families and loyalist families. My father hasn't spoken to me since I was arrested. It took my mother five years before she came to visit me in the Kesh. We could be pushed into the republic and they still wouldn't do anything. The police and the army were losing. Republicans were bombing and killing all over the place. We were on our way out. The only hope was the loyalist paramilitaries. I joined. I felt I'd no choice other than to join.'

'Did you have any formal educational qualifications upon leaving school?'

EDUCATIONAL QUALIFICATIONS

During the interviews, because a number of men with educational potential had left school to pursue trade apprenticeships, the scope of this question was extended to include vocational qualifications. In the loyalist community education was given a low priority – only 20 per cent of the group held qualifications. Men's work was invariably regarded as physical, tough and generally grim, and there were notions of education being a 'soft' option, alien to the extreme macho culture of loyalism. Attainable professions like social work, nursing, community work and teaching were regarded as women's work, banished to the female domain. Ironically it was only in prison that some of the men realised their educational potential, a number studying for and obtaining university degrees.

'Were you in employment at the time of the offence?'

EMPLOYED

'Did you have secure employment prior to the offence?'

SECURE EMPLOYMENT

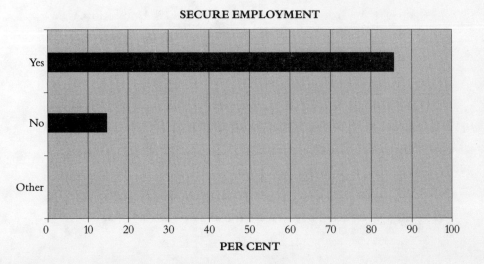

It has been established that there is a high correlation between crime and unemployment. Factors of deprivation, inequality, social exclusion, boredom and social alienation, largely created through unemployment, are usually central to motivation in criminal acts, crime and offending. By any conventional criminal criteria, then, the research group was atypical, given that 90 per cent of the sample were in employment (85 per cent in secure employment) at the time of their arrest. An invitation to the men to comment on the issue of employment threw up some unexpected responses:

'We found it very hard to "keep up" with the Provos. Most of our men were employed, with one or two jobs. We didn't have the time to train properly, to do practice runs, undertake surveillance or reconnaissance. We just didn't have time for the intelligence work vital to successful counter-terrorism. Accordingly, the only time we could operate was on a Sunday, and even then some of the men went to church on a Sunday night. It wasn't long before the Provos caught on to this, and they must have moved South on Sundays, because we couldn't find them. We got just whoever we could, and of course we made mistakes, we were largely untrained part-timers. It used to irritate me going into a bar after a mission. It would come over on the news – an attempted loyalist assassination goes wrong, Catholic man escaped with a leg wound. Some one would invariably say, bloody loyalists, they never get it right. I felt like giving him the piece [gun] and saying, Right, if you can do better, go out and do it.'

'The Provos were full-time professional terrorists – all they had to do was lie in bed, claim British benefits, and go out and kill British citizens. We were paying bloody tax to finance their full-time terrorism. They took our money first, and our lives secondly. If our boys had been full time there wouldn't have been a contest. We would have nailed them.'

'Employment is central to the Protestant psychology, I suppose. What you do defines who you are. It is the Protestant work ethic. The biggest employer on the Falls was the British social security, who financed a political and military war machine, Sinn Féin and the IRA. The loyalists stood on their own two feet, provided for themselves and their families first, and took on the IRA in their spare time. We have very different cultures, and we are defined by those cultures. A first symptom of any impending war will be Protestants leaving their jobs and claiming benefits. If we ever really have to take them on, we'd be prepared, trained, disciplined and methodical, business-like – it's the Protestant way.'

'Work was central to the Protestant way of life. It gave you respect. Respect is very important to Protestants. It's funny, I wouldn't speed to get a ticket through breaking the law, but I went out and killed men. I saw one thing as criminal, and the other as my duty to my people. They [the Protestants] were getting shot and bombed to hell. If we didn't hit back, they would have been wiped out, and yet, by and large, they didn't support us. We offended their notion of respectability. They must have reasoned that it was preferable to suffer and die quietly like the bloody Jews in World War II. Then [their] fate wouldn't have been dissimilar, the only difference was we shot the SS who were intent on our extermination. If it came right to the wire, it would have been them in camps, not us . . .'

'The trouble got so bad in —— I had to give up work, essentially to protect my family. The brew didn't accept that as "reasonable grounds" for leaving work and I didn't receive any benefits for six weeks. Our neighbours gave us food and coal, and "the boys" kept me in cigarettes and drink. We were never so well off. Some of the other boys gave up work and went "full time" as well, to ensure the daytime safety of the estate. There was no way I could have settled in work, knowing that my wife and children were IRA targets in my absence.'

'I gave up work to become active, a full-time soldier. I went down to the social security office to make a claim and the wee girl asked me, "What's your usual occupation?" I laughed and said, "Loyalist travelling gunman." She went pale and ran away to get the manager. Even the dogs in the street knew who I was, but it took them years to get me.'

When asked about the circumstances of paramilitary involvement, all the men replied that they were politically motivated and had joined their organisations voluntarily, with no thought of personal gain or gratification.

'Did you become involved in the offence for personal gain?'

PERSONAL GAIN

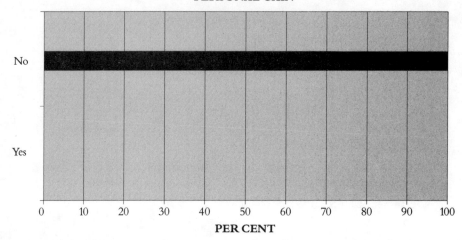

'Did you become involved in the offence for personal gratification, i.e., did you enjoy your involvement?'

PERSONAL GRATIFICATION

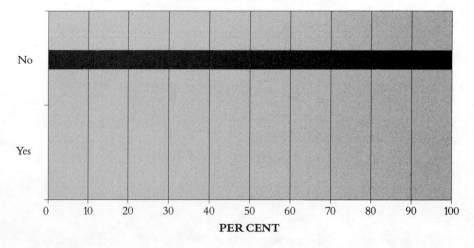

'Did you volunteer yourself into paramilitary involvement?'

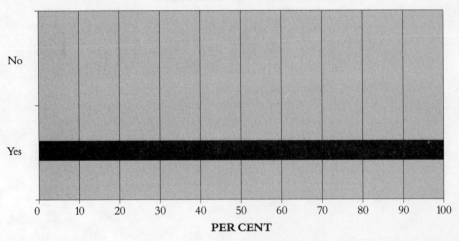

'Did you willingly participate in the offence?'

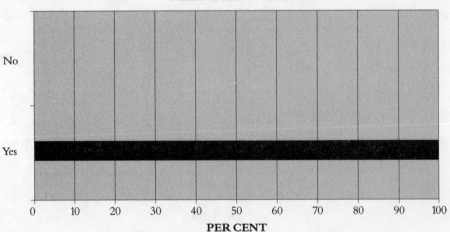

'Was the motivation for your offence criminal?'

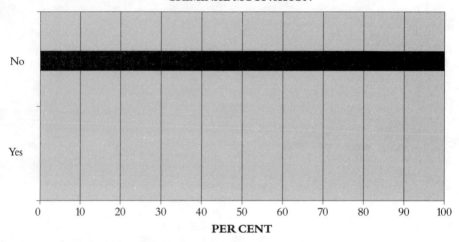

'Was the motivation for your offence political?'

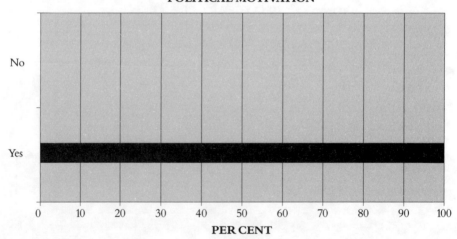

When the former prisoners were asked if their motivation was reactive, the unanimous response included the following representative comments.

'Was the motivation underlying your offence reactive, i.e., against the IRA/republicans?'

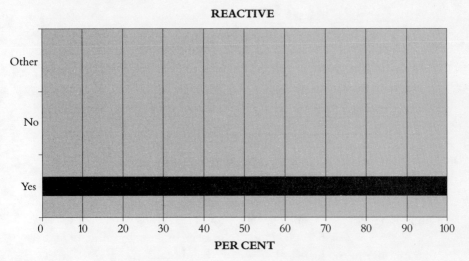

REACTIVE

'Yes, we were reacting against republican violence; we didn't start it. It was counter-terrorism.'

'It's very simple. If the IRA hadn't been at war with us, the UDA would never have been formed. We were formed out of vigilante groups, set up to defend our districts from IRA attack. The RUC and the army had demonstrated that they were incapable or unwilling to defend us. I didn't want to become involved in the paramilitaries, to either end up crippled, dead or in prison. I got involved because I had to. We were all the same.'

'In the early days it was all IRA violence, shootings and bombings. People would ask, Where the fuck are the loyalists? The IRA violence was just getting worse. They had no incentive to stop it. They were winning hands down. They had bombed their way to face-to-face meetings with Whitelaw. The British wanted out. If we didn't stand up for ourselves, they would have pulled out. We had to demonstrate that we were a force to be reckoned with as well.'

'When we started hitting back it was the ordinary Catholics who would put pressure on the IRA to scale things down. It was the ordinary Catholics paying the price, as ordinary loyalists had paid the price, and they didn't like it any more than we did. We knew all about the psychology of terror, we had endured it for long enough.'

'Look, make no mistake about it, it was loyalist guns and bombs that brought the IRA to the negotiation table. They wanted peace all right – they wanted fucking peace from us.'

'The Provisionals had declared war on us. It was the loyalists getting shot and bombed. If their war was with the British, it must have been with the British loyalists, that is to say, the Protestants. From a Provo viewpoint it always was a sectarian war, a war of attrition against the loyalists and unionists. This business about a war of independence against the British was a load of bullshit. It was us they were after.'

'We saw the British doing nothing. They were letting the loyalist people down. It's true to say they were standing back and letting them die.'

'We had a young fella in our estate. He was eleven but had a mental age of five. He would run messages for all the old pensioners and they'd give him money for sweets and chewing gum. He was always chewing. He and another young fella went out of the estate looking for something the local shops mustn't have had. They [the republicans/IRA] captured them and shot them both. They put —— in the boot of a car, poured petrol over it and set it alight. He survived, but it took him five days to die. I was the local commander of the —— battalion, —— Belfast. I called the men together in a local community hall. I said, Volunteers, I have a very serious statement to make. Everyone cheered. They knew what I was going to say. We became active.'

'I'd been walking down the Crumlin Road heading into town and I'd stopped to talk to a young soldier outside the Mater hospital. He was a nice young fella. He told me he'd joined the army to get a tan – he'd hoped to get posted to Cyprus, like a friend of his. Next thing I knew – bang, bang, bang. Half his head was blown off. They [the IRA/republicans] had shot him from a passing car. I dragged him into the hospital screaming and half crying for help. He was still alive; I was in the waiting room. Then it came over on a police walkie-talkie – the young soldier at the Mater, that's now a murder inquiry. I walked out of that hospital a changed man. Something had died in me. I knew I could never be the same again. And that was only the start of it. I've picked bodies, and bits of bodies, bits of children's bodies, children I knew, from bombings in the Shankill. After one particular bombing I went home, and Ma called me in for tea. I said, There'll be no tea tonight, Ma, I've work to do. That was the start of it.'

'At the time it was reactive. I grew up in a stable world. I thought we were all born equal. I had a Catholic girlfriend and I couldn't understand why I couldn't take her home to the Falls "because I was a Protestant". Then the republican's started fucking up the country. I was in Cornmarket on Bloody Friday [Friday 21 July 1972, PIRA set off 26 explosions in Belfast. Eleven people were killed and 130 injured]. It was obvious that the security forces had lost control. I tried to join the police but I was too small. Later that day I joined the UVF.'

'I grew up in the loyalist/unionist tradition. The feeling was, something had to be done. They had to be stopped. All the Protestant businesses were being blown up, and Protestants killed. I had a lot of advantages in life, unlike a lot of the loyalists doing the fighting. I felt there was an onus upon me.'

'We were literally fighting for survival. My "crime" was defending the ordinary decent loyalists, who were undefended and at the mercy of the IRA. That's the way it was.'

'My involvement was essentially defensive. About half my class in school have been killed by the IRA/republicans. A lot of them had joined the security forces. There was a feeling that the IRA could act at will in killing Protestants.'

'[I joined] because of the litany of offences against the loyalist/British community. La Mon [a hotel outside Belfast which was destroyed by PIRA fire bombs in February 1978, killing 12 people and injuring 23]; 3 Scottish soldiers killed; and a boy blown to pieces. More specifically the killing of a 17-year-old retarded boy, taken from his place of work, and shot by the IRA.'

'I was reacting to the systematic destruction of Northern Ireland. The security forces were obviously losing. There was a fear of the Protestant way of life being destroyed. The disbanding of the B Specials [Protestant reserve police force] was the last straw.'

'Were members of your family killed by the IRA/republicans, prior to your offence?'

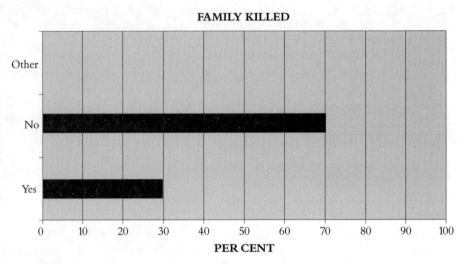

FAMILY KILLED

Thirty per cent of the group responded that members of their family had been killed by the IRA/republicans:

'An uncle of mine was shot by the IRA. He lived for a few months before dying from his injuries.'

'Yes, a cousin of mine was murdered in a sectarian killing.'

'I had a brother-in-law shot, riddled to pieces. He was in the RUC. My brother was also in the police. He had to flee the country after murder attempts.'

'I had a cousin killed. He had been a local councillor.'

'I had a cousin killed. He was a civilian, wasn't involved in anything. He was shot in work on the Springfield Road. A Catholic workmate tried to stop them – he got shot as well. You have to respect him for what he tried to do.'

'I had two uncles killed and one injured.'

'I've had six family members killed since the Troubles. My father and his two brothers were "blown up" in the original Shankill bomb in 1971 [Four Step Inn bombing]. One uncle died, and my father and his other brother were badly injured. My father has never been the same since. Are you supposed to forget about that? It's a bad day in Brighton when the sun doesn't come out. It's a bad day in Belfast when human blood trickles down the drains in the street.'

'Were friends of yours killed by the IRA/republicans, prior to your offence?'

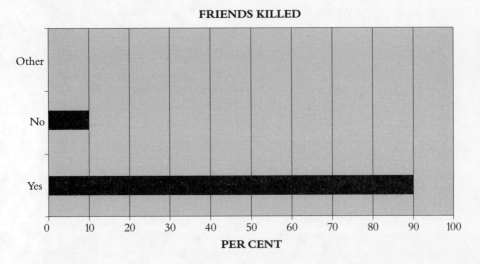

FRIENDS KILLED

'Were members of your home community killed by the IRA/republicans, prior to your offence?'

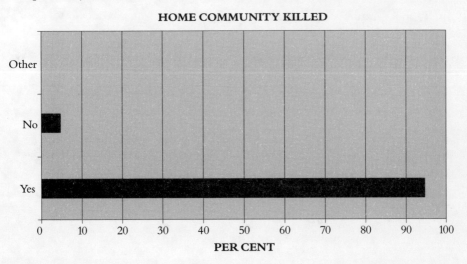

HOME COMMUNITY KILLED

Ninety per cent of the respondents reported that they had had friends killed by the IRA/republicans, and 95 per cent reported that members of their wider community had been killed. One man reported that 10 of his friends had been killed, and 40–50 people in his wider community had died.

'Several of my friends were killed. Loyalist bars in the Woodvale were getting blown up all the time.'

'Four of my mates were killed. My best friend's father was shot dead. We both joined after that.'

'Three of my personal friends were killed, both bombed and shot.'

'I saw women and children blown up on the Shankill.'

'We have lost more people in the Shankill than anywhere else. When I was eighteen I had to pull dead people out of a bombed premises. It was like a nightmare from hell, and I was in it.'

'People I grew up with were killed in sectarian murders. Wrong place, many times.'

'Ten maybe more, good personal friends. People, who were not involved, shot from passing cars, et cetera.'

'A lot of my area was burned down. You couldn't walk down the road. There was fighting every night. And yet before 1968 there had been good community relations.'

'Our community was constantly under bomb and gun attack, and murder attempts.'

'Six good friends killed by the IRA.'

'At the time of your arrest did you think that your offence was advancing the loyalist cause?'

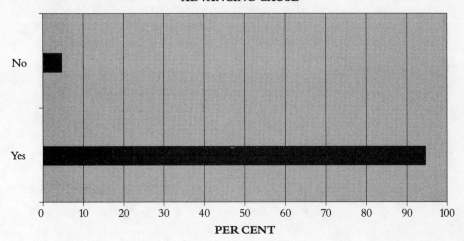

'At the time of your arrest did you think that your offence was in defence of the Northern Ireland state?'

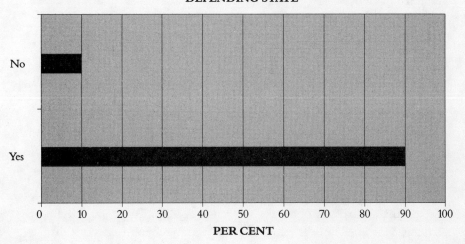

'Do you now feel that loyalist "terror" was instrumental in bringing about an IRA cease-fire?'

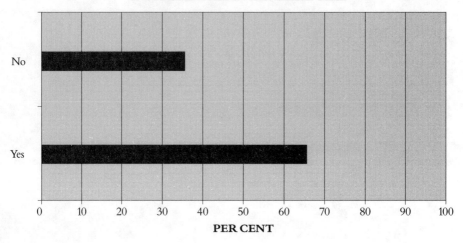

SixtyFive per cent of the respondents felt that loyalist 'terror' was instrumental in bringing about the IRA cease-fire in 1994:

'Most definitely. Without loyalist counter-terrorism we would be in a united Ireland.'

'Without the loyalist paramilitaries we would be in a united Ireland. Even the Provos told us that.'

'No doubt about it. Basically the Roman Catholic community stopped the IRA, because they had suffered so much.'

'If the British taught us anything, that was "violence pays".'

'It was very basic – we got hit; we hit them. We were getting better all the time. Hitting the right people. They knew it. After 1992 we turned the heat up. Thirteen Sinn Féin councillors were killed. We shot up ——'s house. He came on TV. He was fucking terrified, you could feel it. So that weekend we shot his house up again. We knew that he would carry the fear straight into the Sinn Féin leadership. They would feel it, taste it and smell it. Psychologically that was much more effective than just killing him. They called their cease-fire shortly after that [PIRA announced a cease-fire in August 1994]. We were intent on wiping them out, and we were wiping them out, and they fucking knew it.'

'We were very aware of the fear in the Catholic community at large.'

'Yes, without equivocation. I would be more moderate in my views now, now that I know more about Irish history. Education played a part in our failure to understand each other. There were injustices, but it was not by my class or my people. My class did not have the resources to discriminate against anyone. At that time, however, I viewed republican violence as inexplicable and unjustified. What they were doing to us was completely out of proportion with anything which we could possibly have done to them.'

Of the 35 per cent who felt that loyalist 'terror' was not instrumental in the IRA cease-fire, some gave these responses:

'Don't you believe it. They have got a business plan worked out for the next ten years.'

'The so-called peace is tactical. They'll go back to war when it suits them.'

'I honestly believe they will resort to a burnt-earth policy - wipe themselves and everybody else out – to achieve their long-term objectives.'

'Would you buy a used car from them?'

'They are galvanising a political power base before going back on the offensive.'

'There will never be peace. Everybody has lost too much. There has been too much pain and suffering in both communities for either to give an inch on the big issues.'

'At the time of your arrest did you believe that your community (not just the RUC, army, et cetera) was under attack by the IRA/republican movement?'

TOTAL COMMUNITY

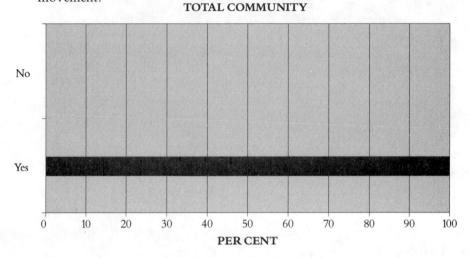

All the respondents felt that their community was under attack by the IRA/republicans, that is to say, they believed that this was not a war being waged between the IRA and the British but a republican war against the loyalist/unionist community in Northern Ireland.

'At the time of your arrest did you believe that the constitutional position of Northern Ireland was under threat because of the IRA?'

CONSTITUTION UNDER THREAT

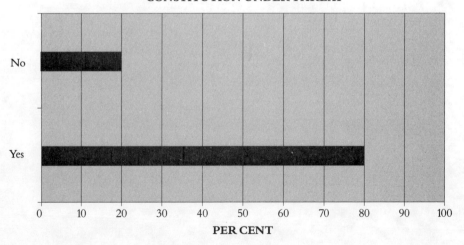

Eighty per cent of the respondents felt that the constitutional position of Northern Ireland was under threat because of the IRA. The remaining 20 per cent also felt that the constitutional position of the state was under threat, not because of the IRA but because of the British disposition towards Northern Ireland.

'Do you think that the Doomsday scenario – open war – is a possibility in Northern Ireland?'

DOOMSDAY SCENARIO

Twenty-five of the respondents felt that a war in Northern Ireland was improbable, and 25 per cent were uncertain. Significantly 50 per cent of this influential and well-informed sample felt that open war in Northern Ireland was probable. No one, however, believed that open war was highly probable.

Discussion

There are many approaches in explaining crime, and in locating and isolating the variables which contribute to individuals committing criminal acts. These can be broadly located in the environment and within the organisation of society (sociological), or can be identified within the individual and the individual's pathology (psychological). Sociologists examine the impact of factors such as unemployment, economic deprivation, structural oppression, lack of social mobility, education and stereotyping. Up to this point my research has examined some of the sociological contributory factors associated with criminal behaviour and it has indicated that the ex-political prisoner group are atypical in terms of expectations which would ordinarily obtain in criminal sociological analysis.

While this approach may be useful, it fails to explain fully why some people do not offend even under the most adverse social circumstances. This failure demonstrates the deficiency of a purely sociological explanation which does not pay due regard to a psychological dimension. Only an approach which combines both can provide a fuller understanding of the individual. The next part of this study, then, was to obtain psychological profiles of my sample group. I did not attempt to psychoanalyse the former prisoners or subject them to a battery of 'psychological' or other 'scientific' tests, which often results in more discussion about methodology than findings. My approach, rather, was based on common sense.

Psychological Profile

'Have you ever been in care?'

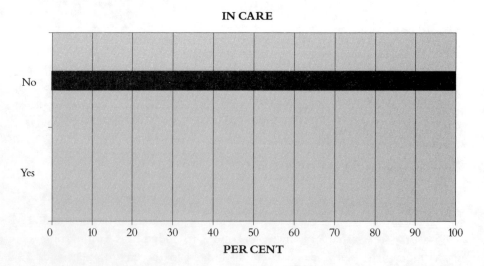

IN CARE

Of the fifty men in the research group forty-nine reported that they had not been in residential children's homes or in social services care. The one exception was a man who reported that he had been in care for a week while his mother was in hospital and his father was working in England.

A 'care' background is common in the assessment of any criminal group.

'Do you derive from a single parent family?'

SINGLE PARENT FAMILY

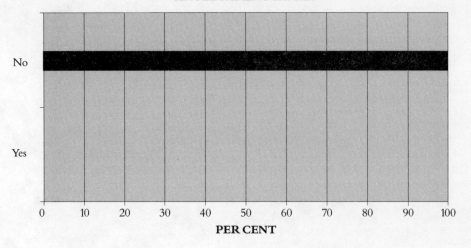

None of the respondents derived from single parent families. 'Single parent families' was explained to mean, the parent was single through choice, circumstance, separation or divorce.

A single parent background is extremely common in the social histories of criminal groups.

Over 90 per cent of the respondents reported 'good' or 'very good' relationships with parents. This fact, perhaps more than any other, establishes the non-criminogenic nature of this group. Bonding, attachment and the establishment of secure parental relationships in early childhood normally determines the nature of the child's (and subsequently the adult's) relationship with the 'outside world'. Almost invariably there is a high correlation between secure relationships in childhood and a stable or normal adulthood. Conversely, where childhood relationships are ambivalent, poor or rejecting in nature, insecurity, self-destructive tendencies and criminality are commonly a consequence. Where poor relationships were recorded, parental alcohol abuse was reported as the causal factor.

'How would you describe your childhood relationship with your mother?'

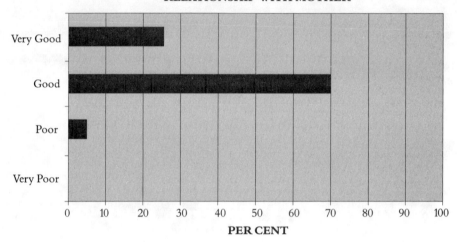

RELATIONSHIP WITH MOTHER

'How would you describe your childhood relationship with your father?'

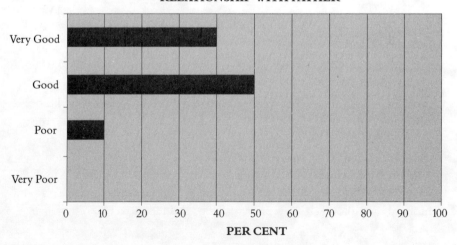

RELATIONSHIP WITH FATHER

'How would you describe your childhood relationship with your brothers and sisters?'

RELATIONSHIP WITH BROTHERS AND SISTERS

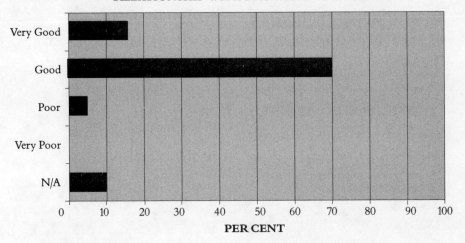

Eighty-five per cent of the group reported good relationships with siblings, with 5 per cent reporting generally good relations, marred only by a strained relationship with a particular brother or sister. Ten per cent of the sample did not have brothers or sisters.

'Did you suffer any form of abuse as a child?'

ABUSE

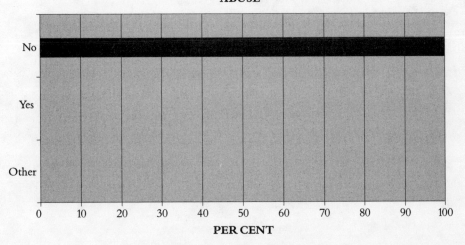

One hundred per cent of the sample reported that they had not been subjected to any form of abuse as children, again setting them apart from any criminal group.

'Did you enjoy primary school?'

ENJOYED PRIMARY SCHOOL

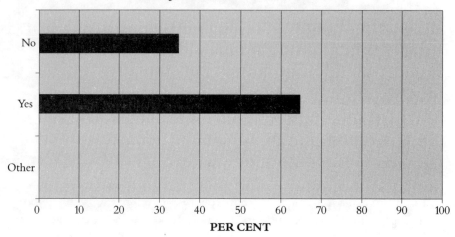

PER CENT

'Did you enjoy secondary school?'

ENJOYED SECONDARY SCHOOL

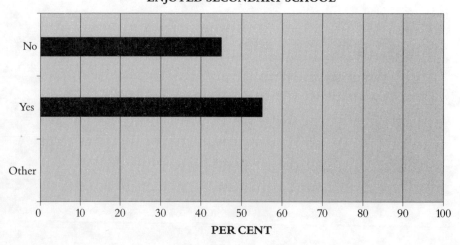

PER CENT

'Did you have a good relationship with a number of teachers at school (primary or secondary)?'

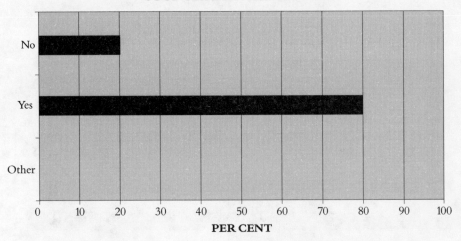

GOOD TEACHER RELATIONSHIP

The experience of school was more variable, with a majority of the sample having enjoyed school; however, a significant number did not. This is probably due to the low priority given to education within the loyalist culture at that time. The cultural ethos was more located in 'getting a job', or 'a trade', than in demonstrating educational competence.

A more significant finding was that 80 per cent of the sample enjoyed good relationships with a number of teachers, a finding which provides insights into attitudes towards, and relationships with, 'rational' authority – another example of a finding which would not be encountered in the analysis of any comparable criminal group.

Of the 20 per cent reporting that they did not have good relationships with teachers, this was attributed to non-attendance, which could be regarded as a fairly well-established norm within the loyalist culture at that time.

Discussion

Even a cursory analysis of the (admittedly common sense rather than 'scientifically' informed) sociological and psychological profiles of the research group sets them strikingly apart from any comparable 'criminal' group. The research data would strongly indicate that the group is a 'non-criminal' sample.

Experience of Imprisonment Profile

'Did you experience imprisonment as dehumanising?'

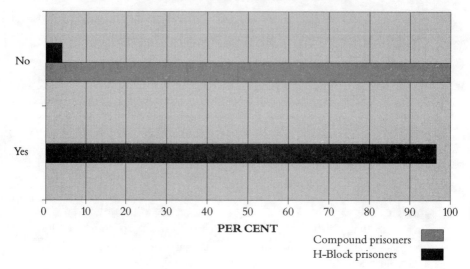

IMPRISONMENT DEHUMANISING

The experience of imprisonment profiles both extend and consolidate the previous findings with regard to the impact of the respective prison regimes: compound (humane containment) and H-Block (punitive). However, there is a significant further dimension to this research as many of the loyalist life-sentence prisoners interviewed had direct experience of criminalisation and suffered the consequences of resisting the implementation of that policy. This includes accounts and evidence from loyalists who refused to wear a prison uniform, choosing instead to 'go on the blanket'. Of the 50 men interviewed, 30 had been imprisoned in the compounds and 20 had been subjected to criminalisation in the H-Blocks.

None of the compound prisoners found the compound system dehumanising and by and large had little comment to make:

'They [prison staff] allowed us to do our own thing. There was no problem.'

'We had nothing to do with the screws.'

'We were answerable to our own leaders. We had our own command structure in place.'

'Doing time is never easy. But we had it real easy, compared to the boys in the blocks.'

'I did fifteen years in the compounds. I'm now in business, self-employed, and doing well. If I'd done fifteen years in the blocks, I'd be a wino on the streets – that's the difference.'

'We knew we were OK compared to the blocks.'

'I actually felt guilty that we had it so easy while some of our men in the blocks were getting their fucking heads kicked in. I wanted to retaliate and go for some of the bastards [prison officers] but it wasn't organisation policy.'

Ninety-five per cent of the H-Block prisoners had experienced their imprisonment as dehumanising. These accounts of the penal system imposed by criminalisation policy are a vivid contrast to the prison accounts of the compound men:

'After I got sentenced I went on the loyalist blanket protest. I was the OC . . . so they [prison officers] left me alone. It was continuous 24-hour lock-up – no exercise, no free association. Cold food, cold tea; even salt, pepper and jam were privileges. I saw a lot of men getting beatings by the screws. They hung one guy, a Provo, upside down and beat him with batons. During the dirty protest the cells got so bad the Provos had to transfer wings. They would have to run through the circle [the centre of an H-Block, which is actually square] and a gauntlet of batons. But I can't say that anything happened to me – they knew better. I heard about other things but I never saw them. I knew that the Provos had hot water thrown over them, really hot water. One of them got a solicitor to take him to court, and he showed the blisters to a magistrate. The magistrate concluded that they were self-imposed – that the prisoner had deliberately stood against a radiator and burned himself, for propaganda purposes. How long would you stand naked against a hot radiator?'

'I was nineteen when I went in. They gave me the uniform and I said I'd rather go naked. I was duly assaulted. I hadn't expected it – no one had told me. They put me on solitary for thirty-five days and beat me black and blue. My mother came to visit and when she saw me she started crying. We forgot all about the IRA; we were now fighting the system. It was a corrupt and brutal system. I went off the blanket because I couldn't take it, but we [the conforming prisoners] weren't much better off. We were continuously beat in the circle for not calling the screws "Sir". It was a borstal system. One day I was taken out for a visit. They had young lads breaking rocks outside the block. I couldn't take it in. Fucking chain gangs. I hated the Provos, but I wasn't into that brutalisation. We felt guilty, lacking in commitment, compared to the loyalist blanket men. I developed an obsessive hatred for screws; I sent messages out. Shoot more fucking screws. They said it wasn't organisation policy. The loyalists had no proper command structure. We felt badly let down.'

'I was among the first batch of loyalist blanket men to go to the blocks. It was frightening, brutal. A line of screws beat you with batons on the way in. Then it was, name – *thump*, full name – *thump*, full name, Sir – *thump*. It's hard to describe what it does to you. It degrades you as a human being and somehow you lose part of your humanity. When I went to prison I thought I hated the IRA, but I didn't know what hate was. I was consumed with hatred. I advocated killing screws. I thought about killing screws, splattering their blood over a wall . . . I know now that I was psychologically disturbed. That's what they did to me. It was even worse for the Provos. Orderlies spitting on their food, ammonia thrown into the cells so that they couldn't breathe. Some of the loyalists nearly cracked up just listening to the screams from the Provo wings.'

One man who had experience of both the compounds and the H–Blocks commented:

'The blocks were the exact opposite to the compounds. In the compounds you had individuality – you were allowed to be an individual. In the blocks you were a prisoner, just a prisoner at the mercy of the screws. They were bastards. They'd be nice to you in the morning and then come back after lunch with a load of drink on. *Thump*. They had to prove that they were the big men, real hard. The blocks made me hard, aggressive, filled with hatred at the abuse and the injustice. They called this a model prison, it must have been modelled on hell. The terrible thing was you lost all sense of responsibility. You actually did become dependent upon the system you hated, because it became your life. There was still some vague sense of who you were, but the system somehow took something from you. Your soul? I don't know.'

'I found the Lord in prison, and I think that's largely because I was surrounded by such evil. I have dogs. I would never mistreat or torture a dog. I don't understand why people torture animals, or men, but there was torture in those blocks. They used to knock you about before the mirror searches. They would stick a floor mirror under you, between your legs, after visits to make sure you weren't carrying anything back. Then they'd 'open' and look up your arse. They wore plastic gloves and would stick their fingers in. That was bloody sexual abuse. It was officially sanctioned sexual perversion. I'll swear they enjoyed it. Some of the beatings were terrible. The whole place was freezing and all you had was a blanket. One day they came for me and took me outside the block naked. I was shivering with the cold. They then hosed me with ice cold water for what seemed about twenty minutes. I had actually gone blue and I couldn't control the shaking. I was glad it was water, because I was crying most of the time . . .'

This abuse of prisoners – at will, for no reason and at any time – was designed to instil fear twenty-four hours a day, fear which rendered the prisoners helpless and created a sense of childlike defencelessness. Nakedness, helplessness and 'being washed' were all part of the treatment. In asserting authority as 'parental' authority, and rebellion as 'infantile' rebellion, the underlying objective was to create subconscious regression. The subliminal message was the futility of infantile rebellion: they had lost this protest before, as infants, and, by association, they would lose again.

As a rule prison officer abuse tends to be reactive, disciplinarian, and used to assert their authority – brutal, not clever. It is the underlying psychology of the technique used against these prisoners that gives cause for concern and merits investigation in its own right.

'. . . A grown man, crying. I couldn't help it . . . I do not know if the leadership outside didn't know what was going on, or whether they didn't have the calibre or the brains. All loyalist prisoners should have been instructed, ordered, to go on the blanket – the whole prison would have collapsed. Loyalist conforming prisoners were virtually running the prison, canteens, cleaning, all of it. It shouldn't have been left to individuals to decide whether or not to go on or off the blanket. There should have been an agreed prison strategy between all loyalist factions, with orchestrated protests outside in support. The system would have folded like a pack of cards.'

While this book is not concerned with simply documenting the excesses of mistreatment associated with the blanket protest and dirty protest, two accounts of loyalist blanket protesters could not be omitted. One man commented:

'How did I regard prison officers? Listen, we were at war with the IRA. I would have shot every Provo in that H–Block, but I could never forgive the screws for what they did to them. That might seem funny, but there are certain rules in life about how you treat people, whether they are black, yellow, Hindu, Catholic, Protestant or Jew. I used to dream about killing prison officers . . . I know it sounds crazy now, but that's the way it got to you. Once a month they had to clean our cells, so they took us to the punishment cells. The governor would always ask us first if we wished to come off the protest. I'd always say, my name is ——, UVF volunteer, politically motivated, political prisoner. "Right, take him away." You could always see out of the cells, through cracks and dents in the door. We could hear what was going on, the sharp intakes of air, before the thuds and screams. They would hit them with the scrubbing brushes. "Right, will we wash your wee dick now" – then the screams. "Right, let's have your arse" – then screams. They never treated us like that, because we weren't on the dirty protest. How the Provos took it, I'll never know. One of our men nearly had a nervous breakdown just listening to it. It just went on and on and on, relentlessly.

'I was being escorted back to the cell once when I saw an IRA prisoner getting a bucket of scalding water thrown over him. He was on the floor with the blisters bubbling and the steam rising from his body. Oh, they loved it. The authorities knew what was going on. They were out to break them. The Provos had no choice but to go on hunger strike. They were driven to it. What in hell were they trying to do? If I'd been a Provo, treated like that, I'd be out every night with a machine gun shooting everything British that I came across. Some of the screws didn't agree with what was going on. They would be transferred and were ostracised. Some of them were real bastards. There were two in particular in the block who led the others on . . . After the protests I met some of the dirty protesters in Maghaberry. I was amazed at how they had taken their treatment in their stride. "Forgiveness" is too strong a term, but there was a sort of acceptance of it. I know the way I was then. I would have shot every fucking screw associated with it. I couldn't have lived with myself otherwise. I was deeply ashamed about something which I could never have had any part of.'

Another man said:

'Because we were on protest they sent us to the punishment block once a month. They punished us to get us to come off the blanket. We were in single cells and all you could do was sit there and wait for the beatings. Then the screws would come in and start beating the man in the first cell. You would hear the screams and the thumps. Some of the boys couldn't take it, and they'd beg for mercy and ask to go off the blanket, but the beating just went on anyway. My mate "Billy" was always in the cell next to me. Billy had a bad back and they always went for that . . . It was hard enough listening to the other men, but I couldn't stand it when Billy was getting it. I knew it was twice as bad for him because of his back. I was actually glad when they left him alone and came in for me. It was actually a relief. We used humour to get over it. We'd make a joke of it, "It's a good job that wasn't your da, Billy, he'd really have beaten your fuck in", or "I swear those screws are getting soft, they don't make them like they used to." '

I heard many more accounts of the inhumanity and brutality of the H-Blocks during the period of criminalisation (1976–81) before the hunger strikes took place.

'How would you describe the circumstances of your imprisonment?'

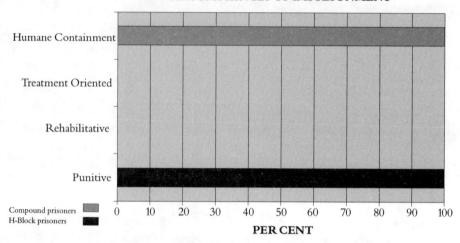

These statistics do not require further elaboration: the compound prisoners felt that they were treated decently, with minimal contact with prison officers; the H-Block group invariably described their experience as punitive, with intensive exposure to staff.

'Did you experience a sense of personal alienation as a result of the conditions of your imprisonment?'

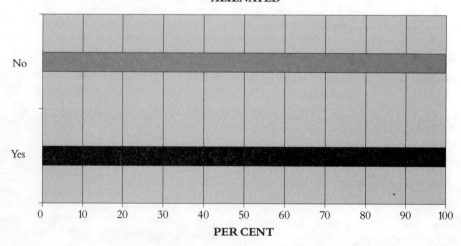

When asked about experiences of alienation the contrast between the two groups was stark: no one in the compound group had experienced aliena-tion, while everyone in the H–Block group reported that they had. One H–Block prisoner commented:

'I didn't know what the word "alienation" meant before I went. It didn't take me long to find out. The beatings, the humiliation, calling those screw scum Sir. The joke is, they call themselves loyalists. I just couldn't understand it. The Provos say they are fighting British injustice and oppression. Then they bring them into prison and subject them to injustice and oppression. They proved to the Provos that the Provos were right in fighting them. If you treat a man like an animal, he becomes an animal; if you abuse him and torture him, over years he becomes your enemy; if you do it to hundreds of men, they become an enemy army, they develop in solidarity each for the other, growing in hatred for the British with every day that passes. I was worried about it, in that it may be the loyalists who have to fight them. The IRA were at war in the H–Blocks. They wouldn't accept criminalisation any more than we would. The morale of the majority of the conforming loyalists got weaker with every day, while the Provos' morale got stronger, as they became more and more committed to their struggle. I could see that as an ordinary fella. What the hell were the British playing at? They were creating a monster for themselves. An élite regiment of the IRA was being formed, in which membership required years of suffering, one for the other, and all for their cause. It was totally around the bend.

'Everybody became alienated in that fucking place, even the screws. They were drinking their heads off. Even if they were half decent sober, they were bastards with drink on. Criminalisation policy fucked up everyone who came into contact with it. I don't know who was responsible for thinking it up, but I'd love to find out. You could see it happen to the new men coming in. They'd be decent, friendly, talking to everyone, and then the reality hit them. They became withdrawn, sullen, angry, bitter, aggressive, always tense, defensive. Presence became very important. You had to assert a violent presence, any weakness was seized upon, either by the screws or other prisoners. I heard one of the prison officials, Minister for Prisons, refer to the H–Blocks as a 'humane containment regime'. That bastard must have spent his childhood in a concentration camp. They would have probably called a concentration camp a rehabilitation centre. God knows what would have been the next stage.'

'How would you describe your relationship with prison officers during your imprisonment?'

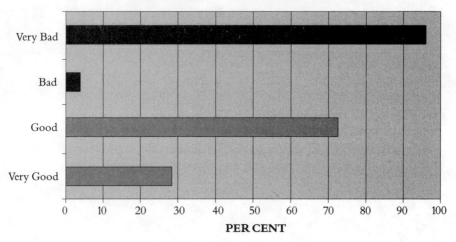

RELATIONSHIP WITH PRISON OFFICERS

When asked about their relationship with prison officers, all compound prisoners reported 'good' or 'very good', while H-Block prisoners reported 'bad' or 'very bad'. Prison officers were seen as the implementors of the institutional (in this case, criminalising) culture and the regulators of the 'pains of imprisonment'. Clearly, the more exposure prisoners have with prison staff, the more they experience that exposure negatively.

'Did your family experience social stigma or rejection in their community because of your imprisonment?'

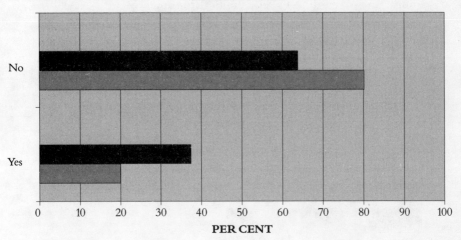

FAMILY STIGMA

'Did you encounter (after release) social rejection or stigma in your community?'

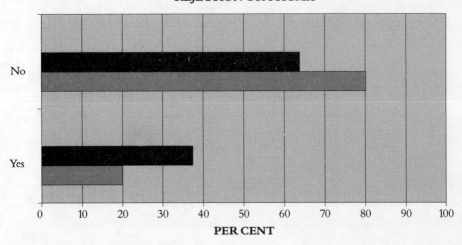

REJECTION OR STIGMA

A majority of prisoners and their families did not experience social stigma as a consequence of their imprisonment – those who did were more inclined to belong to the H–Block group. No doubt this was due to the symbolic linkage with H–Blocks and criminalisation.

These findings also suggest a degree of social ambivalence in unionist communities, regarding loyalist political prisoners. Significantly those men reporting social stigma were more likely to come from 'religious' families, or who would have been lower middle class. In those areas most affected by the conflict – for example, the Shankill – the issue of social stigma did not arise.

'Did the nature of your offence, and your subsequent imprisonment, increase your status in your community?'

INCREASED STATUS

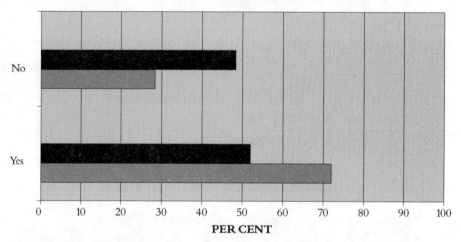

A majority of men reported that their status had increased in their communities because of their offence and imprisonment, once again setting them apart from any comparable criminal group. Some of the men who said that their status had not increased appeared reluctant to answer 'yes', stating rather, 'I did what I had to do. I'm not looking for reward, or respect for it', 'I don't like to think of it in those terms'; 'I don't want another generation following in my footsteps'.

'Did you gain any formal educational qualifications during imprisonment?'

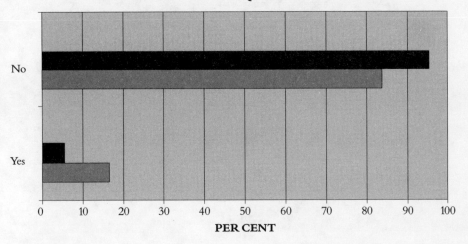

FORMAL EDUCATIONAL QUALIFICATIONS GAINED

Few of the men studied for formal educational qualifications during imprisonment. On the basis of this study, compound prisoners were four times more likely than H-Block prisoners to pursue further and higher education. Some of the compound respondents demonstrated a considerable academic potential and were awarded Open University degrees.

'Did imprisonment increase your level of political awareness?'

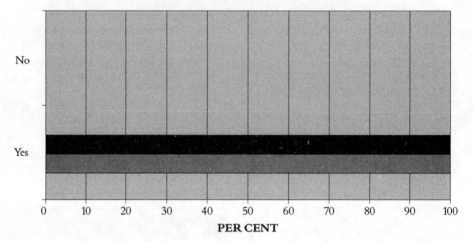

All the respondents, H-Block and compound, felt that imprisonment had increased their political awareness. The men commonly reported knowing 'nothing about Irish history'; 'I knew more about American history'; 'We were just taught to memorise dates of battles'; 'We hadn't a clue about republicanism, or what the hell it was all about. All we knew was that Catholics were shooting at us'; 'We were taught that Catholics had to be kept in their place, otherwise they'd take over'; 'I didn't see it as anything to do with one man, one vote. All I saw was Catholics on our streets, making trouble'.

'Would you say you became politicised during imprisonment (i.e., more inclined towards a political resolution of the conflict)?'

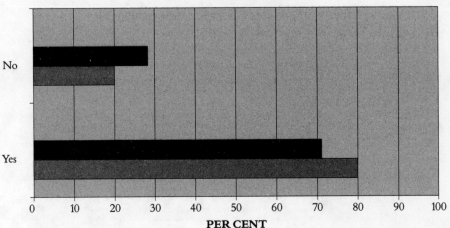

A large majority of the former prisoners interviewed stated that they became 'politicised' during their period of imprisonment:

'I used to think of myself as a soldier at war. They had political education classes in the compounds, and political debates. I used to think they were daft. A soldier doesn't need a political education, he needs a gun. I just wanted to get out, and to get back to the killing. I know now I was wrong, but it was all war, war in those days.'

'The IRA have been at war for nearly thirty years, where has it got them? All those lives ruined, for what?'

'Either we live together, or die together. We need to resolve our differences democratically.'

'We've tried the gun – where did that get us? It got me fifteen years in prison. Ruined my bloody life. We don't need another generation condemned to this.'

'I don't want my children to go through what we went through. I'll talk to anybody to avoid that.'

This change of attitude towards a non-violent, democratic process is reflected in the work of loyalist parties like the UDP and the PUP, which have been supported by the loyalist prisoners.

Re-integration Profile

'Was your release back into the community: very problematic;
problematic; relatively problem free, or problem free?'

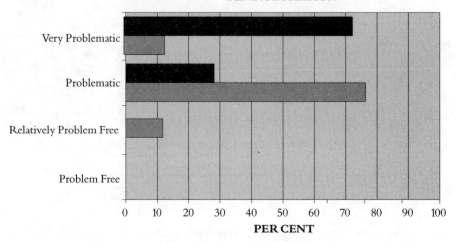

'Could you have benefited from support services during your period of
re-adjustment?'

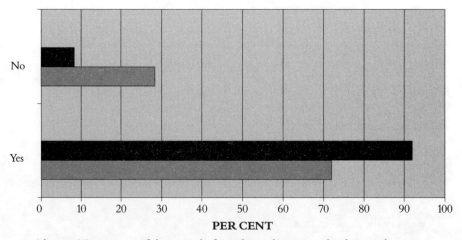

Almost 95 per cent of the sample found re-adjustment back into the community, 'problematic' or 'very problematic'. In particular, former H-
Block prisoners found re-integrating back into the community

extremely difficult, some experiencing mental distress.

In their research into post-release welfare, White, Duffy and Crawford (1997) found that loyalist prisoners do not accept help from the existing statutory and voluntary agencies, which deal principally with criminal populations. The existing loyalist prisoner welfare groups, which operate voluntarily, require a level of resourcing that would allow for expansion and professional training for their volunteers.

Something that cannot be conveyed through the research data, but which merits comment nevertheless, was the physical appearance of the men who took part in the interviews. The compound men presented as normal and were very open in conversation. Trust was quickly established. In contrast, trust took longer to establish with the H-Block men. They needed strong reassurance that I had no link with officialdom, which they had learned to hate. The H-Block men would enter the room bowed, their eyes would dart around the room, taking in all the visual information they could; eye contact would be initially difficult to establish. There was a nervousness and the hushed tones of covert dialogue. These men had suffered too much.

Discussion

Criminalisation policy inevitably involved oppression – the direct oppression of loyalist and republican political prisoners. The policy was an offensive against those who were the most vulnerable, the prisoners, who precisely because of their vulnerability held power in the hearts and minds of people within their communities. The inhumane treatment of the protesting prisoners would forge a contract of unity between the prisoners, and their families, friends and communities.

Interviews with Ex-prison Officers
1998

The former prison officers who volunteered to take part in this research have placed themselves at considerable risk. Every precaution has been taken to ensure their anonymity.

In empirical research, researchers are dependent upon sources of data which confirm or discount the validity of the evidence being presented. In this research, loyalists, republicans and 'ordinary' criminal offenders have volunteered information which has provided for a 'contextual validation' of the evidence presented, in that each of the groups interviewed provided broadly similar responses to most of the questions. Having presented and considered the data from the two principle respondent groups – loyalist and republican former political prisoners – it is now possible to consider data from a third distinct, and highly significant group – prison officers. This will provide for virtually irrefutable evidence within the context of action research.

I had not considered approaching either prison officers or the Prison Officers' Association, as I had assumed that they would be too defensive, or too hostile, to contribute to my research. Quite unexpectedly, however, I was given a contact – a former prison officer who had heard about my study and who wished to be interviewed. He, in turn, referred me to two other former officers who were prepared to be interviewed. In research terminology this is referred to as 'snowballing', where one research contact leads to another. At certain times in empirical research which involves sensitive or even dangerous subjects, such referrals are the only feasible way of contact.

An informal methodology was employed in this part of the study –

the ex-prison officers were simply asked a limited number of key questions. Otherwise the method was to verbally and nonverbally assist the men in the 'telling of their story'. The approach was basically to record oral histories.

Prison Officer One

How long did you serve in the Northern Ireland Prison Service?

I was a member of the service from —— (1970s) until —— (1980s).

Did you have direct working experience of the compound system, the H-Block regime, and the attempted criminalisation of political prisoners?

Yes, all three.

As a prison officer, how did you view the compound system as a form of imprisonment?

We had generally good relationships with the prisoners. We would have been on first name terms with them. The PIRA and UVF, in particular, were very well disciplined; there was never any trouble with them. The UDA were a bit different. There was always a risk of them becoming physical. You have to remember there would only have been four prison officers guarding 80–100 prisoners in each compound. The only thing between you and them was the compound wire. They could have come over at any time. However, the prisoners, and the prisoners' leaders, knew it was in their interests to make it work, so they played by the rules and generally there was no problem. That's why the prisoners were so angry when the government introduced criminalisation. They had played by the rules to keep Special Category status for all those years, and their reward was criminalisation. There was a lot of anger about that. They didn't rock the boat and they felt that they were being punished for something they didn't do. It was a good system; it worked. We would even share cigarettes with the prisoners. In the social club at night nobody talked much about the prisoners, and some officers even boasted about how well they got on with loyalist or republican OCs. By and large we felt we were well off, no hard work, no hassle, and good money, great holidays. You couldn't beat it in the summer, out in the fresh air, sitting out beside the bunk getting a tan.

How did you view the H-Blocks as a form of imprisonment?

Everything changed in 1976. I was sent to H–Block 6. A senior officer there was a psychopath. He had selected an 'élite' band of 'hard men' officers and had obviously trained them for what was to be the new regime. I was sent over from the compounds, a so-called 'compound man'. A lot of us were viewed as soft, because we had no experience of 'real prison'. I couldn't believe what was happening. As the prisoners were brought into the block the vans arrived at the front of the H–Block. The prisoners expected to get out. Then the vans drove around to the back. I couldn't understand that. The prisoners, many of them only seventeen and eighteen, seemed to sense something was wrong, and they were right. Prison officers were lined up all along the wing, and the prisoners had to run the gauntlet. Prison officers used their batons and the straps of the batons to beat the prisoners, and some officers kicked them. These were the 'super screws' and this was obviously the new model for the officers in the H–Blocks. This was the new culture of criminalisation, the Northern Ireland Office's latest brainchild. Personally, I was convinced that prisoners treated in this way, so badly, would be bound to become so bitter that they would re-offend. They are expected to follow the rules, as we break every rule in the book?

A senior officer would interview the prisoners individually. They would be called into the middle of the circle and would have to stand to attention. One prison officer would stand behind the prisoner, two at either side, with the senior officer in front. He'd give them dog's abuse, screaming at them and slapping them. The other officers would also shout. If a prisoner relaxed, he got a thud in the back. If he spoke, he got slapped or thumped from either side. The idea was to break down the prisoners' defences, to let them know who was in charge, and that they could do any bloody thing they wanted.

The prison officer ethos in the blocks was that of hard men, and the harder you were, the more status and respect you got [within the prison officers' culture]. Conversation had changed in the social club: a lot of it was about work and prisoners – who was asking for it, who was going to be put down, who they were going to get.

Prisoners would go from their cells to the circle to see the medical officer. On one occasion in the early days a class officer came out and stopped this young prisoner, and demanded to search him. He told him to take his boots off. That was ridiculous and the prisoner knew it, so the prisoner hesitated. The screw behind me said, Right, I'm going to get that fucking cunt. I stopped him and that was me a marked man. I wasn't one of them any more. The prisoner stared at me and gave me a nod. That meant he was going to report back [report an account of the incident to the IRA's H-Block leadership]. I had acted spontaneously; the significance of what I had done never occurred to me at the time.

The prisoners were strip-searched, I mean, internally searched. Christ, you could never be the same after that. The bastards enjoyed it.

Were you involved in work with prisoners protesting against criminalisation?

Blanket protest – that's when the sadists really came into their own. The prison officers, the hard men. The prisoners were really the hard men; they just took it and said nothing. I couldn't believe just what they were prepared to sacrifice and endure for what they called 'status'. The protesting prisoners refused to wear a criminal uniform. They weren't allowed out of their cells unless they wore a uniform, so they couldn't slop out the chamberpots in the wing toilet. A trolley came round and they slopped out into that. That worked fine. Then they – the Northern Ireland Office, or prison department, I don't know – decided to stop the trolley round to force the prisoners to wear the uniform, to go to the wing toilet to slop out. The republicans refused, and that started the dirty protest. The protesting loyalists continued to slop out, but refused to wear the uniform. The PO [principal officer] of the H-Block wouldn't even allow them to wear a towel around their waist. They had to undergo abuse and humiliation each and every time they slopped out.

The prisoners only wore a uniform once a month to take their visit. They were strip-searched. Strip searches are a common procedure in UK prisons. Prisoners are taken to a room for privacy and strip-searched – top half first and then bottom half – to avoid undue humiliation to the prisoner. In the blocks they were stripped completely and spread-eagled over a mirror for everyone to see. They would be internally searched. If they resisted, which was the natural human response, the visit was refused or they were beaten into submission.

Did you witness any other abuses of prisoners?

Oh yea. Buckets of boiling water being taken down the wings, and I mean boiling water. They would kick open the cell doors and throw the boiling water over the prisoners. They [the prisoners] really had to rough it in the winter. It was freezing. They [the prison officers] would use hoses. They'd put them through the windows and hose the prisoners, mattresses and everything, and leave them to freeze. They would shout, You're only fucking vermin. And that's what they believed.

Something big was going on there. They [the Northern Ireland Office/government] were trying to bring about anarchy. Traditionally, prisoners are the most important part of the so-called republican movement. If you take on the prisoners, even one prisoner, you take on the entire republican movement, and by that I mean the IRA. And here we were torturing them, not one or two of them, but hundreds of them. The attitude was, 'hammer them into submission', but we knew they were never going to break. When the Provos shot —— I was actually glad. He was a Catholic, and yet he had been one of the most cruel officers to his own kind. He had provided a role model for brutality, a real bloody sadist. One of the other screws I knew from the compound days said, 'I was sorry to hear about —— getting shot.' I just said, 'That fucking bastard had it coming.' He didn't look surprised – despite what he had said, he'd obviously thought the same thing. He walked on; there was nothing else to say.

The loyalists were laughed at. Nobody really took them seriously. There was a *Belfast Telegraph* headline one night, 'Loyalist Prisoners Go On Hunger Strike', then the next night, 'Loyalist Prisoners End Hunger Strike'. They saw the British as their friends. They had no idea about how to respond to what was happening in 'their' prisons. If they had all gone on blanket protest, the place would have ground to a halt. The loyalists were used to service the prison, to do all the jobs. Even more importantly, all the prison officers lived in loyalist areas. If we had been really threatened [by loyalists], the POA [Prison Officers' Association] would have intervened and the protest would have been resolved.

One former political protesting prisoner informed me that he had been taken outside an H-Block and, in the middle of winter, hosed, naked, for twenty minutes. Is that possible?

Not only is that possible, it happened. The screws regarded the prisoners as scum bags; they called them 'fuck dogs'. They didn't see them as human beings, so they didn't care what they did. The blanket men had one half-hour visit per month. That was the only time they could have a cigarette. The prisoners would light up on the visit. The officers would let them get the first couple of drags, to get a taste for it, then they would make them put the cigarette out. If prisoners were appealing their sentence, they were also entitled to an appeal visit of fifteen minutes' duration per month. It was decided that all they could talk about was business related to the appeal. So if your wife and children came up, all you could talk about was the appeal. This was brutal. I was there one time when a prisoner's wife and two young children came in for their visit. The young boy shouted, Daddy, Daddy, I got a first in class. The officer jumped up: Right that's it, visit over. You should have seen that child's face. He was going to remember that day for the rest of his life.

On another occasion two elderly parents had travelled down from Derry to see their son on the appeal visit. The mother smiling at seeing her son said, God son, it's cold in here. The officer shouts, God has nothing to do with this. Visit over. A father came in to see his son and said, Liverpool were on last night; the visit was brought to an end so abruptly the poor bastard [the prisoner] never got to hear the score.

The prison officers had a weekly competition about who could end an appeal visit quickest. The screws didn't agree with prisoners having this concession. It was their legal right, but the officers ran the prison and the officers were above the law.

The prisoners on protest never got out of their cells and so they had no company other than their cell mate. When you would escort them from the H-Block, they would be desperate for human contact and conversation. A prison van would pass and they'd say, See that prison van, that's a good van. What sort of vans do you like? What was any young fella doing talking about vans? Most of the officers refused to talk to them, but it was so pathetic some did. When the authorities caught on to this, they put two men on appeal visit escorts to ensure that all conversation with prisoners stopped.

That system [criminalisation] changed men. Decent officers I knew from the compound side came to the blocks, and went power mad. I didn't recognise them as the same people I had known. They wouldn't speak to me because I spoke to the prisoners. We all talked to the prisoners on the compound side. Ordinary decent fellas [prison officers], when they went to the blocks they lost their soul, their morality, their spirit, their humanity. But yet, what they had to do, or felt they had to do, went against their true nature. They were acting out the part, the macho-man. A lot of them couldn't cope with it, but they never talked about it. They didn't want to let the side down, they didn't want to appear weak, so they went on doing it without comment or complaint.

You'd see them drinking from bottles of vodka in their cars in the morning before they went in. Nearly all the marriages broke up. Sick leave and alcoholism were rampant. I saw some officers sitting in chairs, vacant, just rocking back and forward. I'm no psychologist, but you just knew that that was serious.

Criminalisation policy and criminalisation in practice contaminated everybody and everything that it came into contact with. It changed people and ruined people's lives, and I'm no exception. Eighteen prison officers dead, and God knows what else, and for what? We'll probably never know the full impact of the alienation caused by that bloody policy. The suffering it caused hasn't stopped. It won't stop for another generation.

Prison Officer Two

How long did you serve in the Northern Ireland Prison Service?

From —— (1970s) until —— (1980s).

Did you have direct working experience of the compound system, the H-Block regime, and the attempted criminalisation of political prisoners?

Yes, I worked in all of those, in loyalist and republican compounds, and in conforming and non-conforming H-Blocks, and with the streakers [prisoners on blanket protest].

As a prison officer, how did you view the compound system as a form of imprisonment?

When I first saw the compounds I thought they were like large cages with men inside. I thought to myself there must be a more constructive and humane way of holding men. God, had I a lot to learn about imprisonment. The prisoners didn't hate us there. The first thing they learned to do in the H-Block was to hate us. They hated us because of what some of us did to them, and I could fully understand why they hated us. In the compounds, life was fairly relaxed and easy going, you didn't have to fear for your life then. In the H-Blocks there was hatred and a constant intensity that was more like going into a war zone than taking a dander around the compounds. You would get the odd bit of abuse – name-calling, a stone thrown at you – but always from a distance. The big difference was, in the compounds prisoners didn't want to kill you or, more accurately, they didn't want to have you killed.

How did you view the H-Blocks as a form of imprisonment?

The first block to open was H–Block 2, and that was brutal. All the staff there were hand-picked hard men, and there were some who were really bad. They got their status in life by humiliating, abusing and terrorising the young prisoners in H–Block 2. The power they held and used over the prisoners made them feel big, important – look at me, I've got power, I'm important. Outside the prison you wouldn't have pissed on them. They were just screws. That's what you did when you could not do anything else. They were men of no consequence on the outside, but they were damn sure that they were going to be of consequence in the H–Blocks.

H–Block 2 was where they held the YPs [young prisoners]. Predictably they wanted to test out the new strategy, criminalisation, on the young lads, as they were the most vulnerable. Having established a base there, they began working their way through the rest of the system. Some of the compound men didn't like it, but the changes were brought about with a ruthless determination. It must have been like Jersey in World War II. One day the British were running things and everything was fine. The next day the Germans were in control, and you couldn't do a thing about it. The POs [prison officers] in the non-conforming [protesting] blocks were hand-picked for their brutality.

Were you involved in work with prisoners protesting against criminalisation?

When the prisoners were on the blanket they were fair game. Some of the prison officers were real bastards, sadists. They were encouraged and rewarded for what they did. There was a silent majority of prison officers who just went along with it. They had mortgages and cars to pay, and wives and children, or girlfriends, to keep. Most of them had never dreamed of earning so much money. I know when I couldn't take it any more and went sick my wife would say, What's wrong with you? Everybody else can do it, why can't you! When I tried to explain she said, Look I didn't join the bloody prison service, you did. You made your bed, now lie in it. When I threatened to resign, she threatened a divorce. The money was just too good. I know a lot of the men were in exactly the same boat.

In the H–Blocks, if you were a dissenter, if you went against the system, you were allocated all the shitty jobs. Gate duty in the pouring rain in the middle of winter at some isolated gate no one used, all the worst shifts, weekend duty. They could even have you transferred to Magilligan [a remote prison in County Derry]. So the ordinary men went along with it – they even pretended to enjoy it. But if they enjoyed it so much, why did they have to get blocked every night, why did they stop going home, why the divorces, the loss of contact with children and families? They were losing their identity. They used to laugh about what they did, but there was a fear. They knew it was wrong. The sheer discipline of the Provos, the silence, and then the screams, and then the deafening silence. Then with a solemn tone, someone would say in Irish, 'Our day will come'. A lot of the young republicans had been brainwashed about British injustice and oppression, and that a Catholic could never get a fair deal in British Ulster. The H-Blocks proved the Provos right. They were getting British oppression. It was being served up to them three times a day, every day, for year after year. The British were playing into the Provos' hands. The Provos hadn't wanted a cushy prison system, like the compounds. They wanted British brutality back in the prisons to win more support and influence in nationalist and republican areas. The hard men of the prison service were too thick to understand what was going on. The prison officers and the prisoners had been set at each other's throats, as pawns, in a bigger game. The prisoners who fought the system survived and won; the prison officers who surrendered to the system lost.

Did you witness any other abuses of prisoners?

There was this loyalist prisoner in H-Block 3. He was a thirty-year man and he had been working at some project in his cell which needed a small screwdriver. This prison officer asked me to accompany him to retrieve it, as the prisoner wouldn't be allowed that overnight. Right, he said, we're going to play hard ball. I said, no, we'd just ask him for the screwdriver. I knew he [the prisoner] had had a bad visit that day – maybe his wife didn't turn up, I don't know, but this was a big thing for the prisoners. The prison officer kicked the cell door open and started to get heavy with the prisoner, knocking him around. The loyalist lashed out with the screwdriver, which was about three inches long, giving the officer a flesh wound on the back. We left. Four prison officers returned to the prisoner's cell, where they beat and kicked him senseless. He was one of only two prisoners I didn't hear squeal when this happened. There was him and ——. Jesus, he was a hard man. He was very badly beaten up. They threw him into the back of a van and took him to the punishment cells. There was no need for any of that.

At one time this doctor in the block decided that the prisoners involved in the dirty protest would have to be bathed. Later on, after the doctor had left, two officers took a streaker from his cell to the washroom. They filled the bath full of roasting hot water and threw the prisoner in. He was screaming. A chief officer arrived on the scene and just watched, smiling. This proved to me that it was all authorised. The prisoner tried to turn on the cold tap with his foot and toes – it was smacked down with a long scrubbing brush. They kept him in by hitting him with the long scrubbing brushes and, when the water cooled, scrubbed him with the ordinary brushes. He came out of the bath roaring red. You would have thought he had some sort of deadly disease.

All of this allowed the Provos to say, this is the real British system, this is what the British will do to you, and to us. The British are without honour, without decency, and without human compassion.

There were two other prison officers I knew. They would put the prisoners going for visits in the transit vans, which had benches running along each side of the van facing each other. They would sit opposite the prisoners and rub their hobnail boots up and down the prisoners' shins, drawing blood. They enjoyed doing that. They thought it was funny. The prisoners had no choice but to take it, or face something a lot worse.

After the hunger strikes everything changed. Suddenly everything became relaxed and liberal. That's when the Provos got their own back. The Provos used psychology to get at the officers. They would stare at them relentlessly. A prisoner would ask a prison officer something on the wing, then he [the prison officer] would be confronted by fifteen of them, all silently staring at him. It's hard to explain the way they looked at you, it was chilling. At night there would be one officer on the wing with everything locked up – it was an evil environment. Someone would shout out the officer's home address; someone else, the make and colour of his car; someone else, the registration number of his car; someone else, his wife's name. That cracked the officer up. This time there was nothing they could do about it. The Provos differentiated between officers – they went for the bastards, the hard men. If you'd been decent to them, they left you alone. Nothing will ever happen to me, I could go and drink on the Falls Road and still be OK.

Prison Officer Three

How long did you serve in the Northern Ireland Prison Service?

All together, about ten years.

Did you have direct working experience of the compound system, the H-Block regime, and the attempted criminalisation of political prisoners?

I had only a short time in the compounds and worked mainly in the blocks. I was there during criminalisation, the protests and the hunger strikes.

As a prison officer, how did you view the compound system as a form of imprisonment?

I worked mainly in the republican compounds. Their discipline was second to none. It was a military operation. They had their own OCs and no one stepped out of line. The UVF were well disciplined as well, thanks to Gusty Spence. The UDA by and large did what they wanted. They were a collection of individuals more than an army. The UVF actually had military drills and inspections in the compounds. The UDA would laugh and jeer at them, but they [the UDA] were the cowboys. In the compounds you were very aware that the prisoners ran the prison. We had very little direct dealings with them, although there was no bad feeling. If they wanted anything sorted they would call for a PO [principal officer] or governor – we didn't have any real power, so there was no point in talking to us. They were always pushing for something – an extra visit for someone, more handicrafts, better food. In the summertime the prisoners sunbathed. You'd go to Spain or somewhere for a fortnight, come back tanned, and there they were, even browner than you. I must admit, I resented that.

How did you view the H-Blocks as a form of imprisonment?

The blocks were a different world. It was hard to believe you were in the same prison. In the blocks prisoners were prisoners, and officers were officers. The prison officers had the power to do whatever they liked and they took full advantage of it.

A lot of the prison officers could handle themselves, they really could, they were fairly hard men. Thank God, I wasn't born a hard man. I had a difficult childhood. My father was a bastard. I suppose I understood what it was like to be abused, and those prisoners were abused. The prisoners

were called animals, shit, crap, scum. The laws of nature didn't apply any
more. These were people who were helpless, without any means of
defence. There was an instruction from somewhere to brutalise these
people. It was the first time a lot of the prison officers had real power, and
it went to their heads like a drug. Call me Sir, stand to attention, strip,
bend over, stand with your hands on the wall. Some of them were
insignificant wee shits treating grown men that way. It was demeaning,
dehumanising, but what the screws didn't realise was that they were
dehumanising themselves. When you rob another human being of
human dignity, you rob yourself of human dignity. In the streaker
blocks, they [the prison officers] got an extra ten pounds, or something, a
day. Their lunch break lasted from 11.30 a.m. to 3.00 p.m. They had
nothing to do only open doors, and literally throw food in.

In the prison service you had no real status, but you could get status in
the blocks by being a bastard. To get the 'respect' of the prisoners. In
reality, all they got was fear and hatred; that was the basis of their power.
It was a macho thing, being the hard man, the harder the better. You
won't believe this one. I overheard two screws talking once during the
tea break. They were talking about women and sex when one of them
said, You know, last night she made me do it with my hat on. Jesus. The
big tough screw, the man in the uniform. I wonder if she realised what it
actually stood for? Yea, she probably did. Sick, isn't it?

The H-Blocks were bad, they were really bad. If men weren't bitter
before they came in, by God, they were when they left.

Were you involved in work with prisoners protesting against criminalisation?

Basically you had two types of prisoner, the politicals and the ordinary
criminals. The ordinary prisoners were conforming prisoners – they
weren't on protest. A majority of the loyalists and a fair number of
republicans were also conforming prisoners, but generally speaking they
were all treated so badly it didn't matter much. I would have worked
mostly with conforming prisoners. The Provisionals started their protest
in 1976 and we knew they had it rough. By 1978 criminalisation policy,
or brutalisation policy, as it really was, was being applied to all the
prisoners.

The first thing I knew about the beatings was when a prisoner asked
me, What do you think of all these beatings? I didn't believe him. I was
there as a prison officer and I hadn't a clue. It just spread over the prison.

The sadistic branch got put into positions of power and everyone took the cue from them. I was put on escort duty for visits with the Provos on protest. Young fellas, most of them. When you got out of earshot from the blocks they'd be desperate to talk to you, to hear news about anything. Football was the favourite, Cliftonville or Celtic. They'd never talk about anything personal, like where you lived or holidays. The Provos had apparently instructed them not to talk to us, as we had been instructed not to talk to them, but they just needed someone to talk to, a good officer. I asked them what was going on and it sounded like a description of hell. Men being beaten, held upside down and beaten, boiling water being thrown over prisoners, prisoners being stood up against hot radiators and burnt. The first time I heard it, it frightened me. I just thought, what in God's name is going on here?

Did you witness any other abuses of prisoners?

We didn't talk about what was going on, we avoided it. I still don't like to talk about it. If you had one or two good friends, you could talk about it. As the prison officers got shot, we pretended we didn't know why – the screw got a funeral and the family got good money from the NIO, and that was the end of the story. I saw likeable, charismatic people, people you would have liked, turn into sadistic, brutal bastards.

During the hunger strike, prisoners got to the stage where they didn't know if they were horizontal or vertical. I saw prisoners who were very ill men crash into things, hit walls, stumble and fall flat on their faces, because no one – no one – would help them. They were 'unclean people', 'terrorist scum', and so they had to make their own way out.

The strip searches were brutal. There were rules about how men should be strip-searched. We were told not to worry about them, they were 'English rules'. The prisoners would be forced to strip and squat over a mirror before their visits. If they refused, they were either beaten into submission or the visit was cancelled. This was deeply resented by the prisoners as it involved abject humiliation, and they were often laughed at and ridiculed. They would be strip-searched in the H-Block in full view of everybody and then they were strip-searched in a hut at the visiting area before they could take their visit. There was no need for that and they knew it, because they were under the personal individual supervision of a prison officer between the block and the hut. My memory is not too clear here, but then I think they were strip-searched in the visiting hut again, before finally being strip-searched in the H-Block after the visit. To me this was worse than the beatings. The beatings were human; this was official, institutional.

There was one principal officer in particular, he was a nice fella, but cruel. He'd say to the protesters, Right, you piss on that floor and you'll lie in it. That's what he made them do. He was a good looking guy, very physically fit. The sadistic branch treated him like a god. They would have built an altar to him if they could. He was leaving one of the blocks, and the other prison officers went to soak him in a bath. That was the custom. There were four big officers who went for him. He beat the four of them off. You can imagine what it was like when he went for a prisoner.

The Provos called it Long Kesh Concentration Camp. There's one thing which I always thought was ironic, where the republicans shot themselves in the foot. The prisoners on hunger strike would be moved to the prison hospital, where they had unlimited access to their families. They [the prisoners] were lying dying, refusing food, all food. The canteen was open for the families, tea and chicken sandwiches, and they always got stuck in. They shouldn't have eaten that food while their prisoners were dying rather than eat. I thought this was ironic, given all the Provos' discipline and attention to detail. It proved to me that this wasn't a family thing, that the ideology did not come from families. These weren't republican families, or if they were, the whole bloody thing was a joke.

After the hunger strikes, the prisoners had won. The hard men got moved away from the prisoners and into administration, or to the carpark, or the censors, or to anywhere where they could do no more harm. Their days had come and gone and not before time. They became ostracised. The prisoners had been through protests, the dirty protest, the beatings, the boiling water, the hoses and then the deaths. They weren't taking any more. The truth is, the prison officers were frightened, they knew it had got way out of control. That's why they drank themselves into oblivion, stopped going home as often, and drove like mad men. They were scared, and their families were scared. They suddenly caught on – they had been used and they were regarded as expendable. When they got shot nobody gave a damn. The whole bloody thing was despicable.

Discussion

By highlighting the merits of the compound system of imprisonment relative to the H-Block regime, the prison officer research complements the prisoner research. Prisoner mistreatment and abuse, which were to become the overriding characteristics of the H-Block system, did not occur in the compounds. The brutality experienced by the H-Block prisoners led to hatred and alienation within that group, which amplified the aggressiveness and hostility of prison officers. The conditions in the H-Blocks of Long Kesh had been contrived in such a manner as to make this an inevitable outcome. It is important to note that the three former prison officers felt that many of their colleagues acted out abusive roles even while regarding them as morally wrong – a source of conflict for many of the more ordinarily 'decent' staff. Nevertheless, there were other prison officers who clearly appeared to relish the opportunity to brutalise the prisoners. Whatever motivation can be assigned to the prison officers of Long Kesh, these interviews indicate a toleration of the staff's mistreatment of prisoners and a belief that covert encouragement was given by the authorities – in short, that these abuses were part of the official policy towards the successful implementation of criminalisation.

Epilogue

When the British government introduced Special Category status in 1972 it implicitly conceded the principle of political, or prisoner-of-war, status to the loyalist and republican combatants. This concession reflected what was in fact the reality for the republicans and the loyalists – they they were fighting a war to determine the future of the Northern Ireland state.

The conditions afforded by the Long Kesh compound system facilitated unique accommodations between the most extreme and uncompromising groups in Northern Ireland society. The inter-relationships forged there were characterised by distinct stages and were paradoxically a direct consequence of the one thing the paramilitaries had in common – conflict. In the confines of the prison the alternative to a no-conflict policy was virtual open warfare, and the subsequent inter-group negotiations to avert a degeneration into violence provided the basis for developing and evolving relationships on matters of common interest, leading to the formation of the camp council which represented all the paramilitary groupings. The proposal of the downtown office scheme represented a willingness, at least on matters of prisoner welfare, to transpose this relationship to the outside world. This was a remarkable achievement and one which should have been encouraged in its development. Many of the participants felt that such paramilitary dialogue and negotiation provided for one possible avenue towards the ultimate prize of peace.

Criminalisation put an end to all of this work. When the policy was introduced in 1976 it transformed conditions in Northern Ireland's prisons and became almost the sole issue and focus of concern for republican and loyalist paramilitaries alike. Special Category status had been

won from the government through hunger strikes and external paramilitary pressure. Not surprisingly, the government's decision to phase
it out was viewed as an act of extreme provocation, which inevitably
led to confrontation – the blanket protest, the dirty protest and the 1981
hunger strike.

The impact of criminalisation policy on prisoners, and prison staff, and
on the communities to which they belonged is revealed in the chilling
accounts of brutality and torture experienced by republican and loyalist
protesting prisoners. These accounts are corroborated by the three ex-
prison officers, whose own stories of incomprehension and horror of
sadistic practices, seemingly sanctioned by the administration, speak for
themselves. A striking feature of some loyalists' testimonies is the degree
of empathy they felt towards their republican counterparts. Loyalists
frequently expressed the view that the republicans were forced into a
hunger strike, and one prison officer felt that 'something big was going
on in Long Kesh, that they [the British] were trying to bring about
anarchy'.

There is no doubt that the prison conditions and the hunger strikes
angered and traumatised much of the nationalist and republican communities in Northern Ireland. The anticipated escalation of republican violence would have drawn fire from the loyalists and the stage would have
been set for open war in the North – a scenario which seemed all too
possible in the dreadful days of 1981. The fully expected PIRA retaliation
did not, however, follow the deaths of the ten republican hunger strikers
– Sinn Féin had elected instead for a political route and for a negotiated
settlement. But it would take a long time for those republicans with political vision to convince the more militant elements of the organisation to
eschew violence and follow their lead.

When PIRA declared a cease-fire and an end to its war on 31 August
1994 loyalists were deeply suspicious that a deal had been brokered
between the Provisionals and the British government. Although both
the UDA and the UVF were given assurances that no deals had been done,
loyalist paramilitaries continued with their violent campaign, many of
the loyalist commanders being reluctant to call their own cease-fire
because they felt that for the first time they could match the
Provisionals' capability in every aspect of the conflict. By now the UVF
had lethal Powergel explosives and the technical expertise to detonate
hugely destructive bombs. One mid-Ulster unit commander actually

stated that the Provisionals were 'no longer a problem' and that 'the fight' should be taken directly to Dublin and the South.

It transpired, however, that the loyalist prisoner population was to have a central and crucial role in the politics of a loyalist cease-fire. The UVF prisoners were generally regarded as a battalion of the organisation, with the same status and power as any other battalion. Accordingly, they would be bound to accept any cease-fire arrangements entered into by the leadership. The UDA operated in a very different way. For them any cease-fire would depend upon the active support of the prisoners, effectively giving them a veto. Advocating a cease-fire, John White of the UDP consulted with UDA and UFF prisoners. His endeavours were so successful that the prisoners wanted to declare their cease-fire in the prison carpark, in advance of the Combined Loyalist Military Command (CLMC) declaration of 13 October 1994. On that date Gusty Spence expressed his remorse for the suffering and the deaths of the innocent victims of the conflict, gave an assurance to loyalists that the Union was safe, and stated that the sole responsibility for a return to war lay with the republicans. In August 1995, seeking to consolidate the cease-fire, the CLMC pledged that there would be no first strike by loyalists, which implicitly invited PIRA to reciprocate – an invitation that has yet to be taken up.

The contribution made to the peace process by the paramilitary prisoners has been played down and often repudiated by a wider society quick to accept the imposed criminal status of Northern Ireland's political prisoners. It must be understood, however, that without prisoner support and agreement the cease-fires would never have come about and the peace negotiations would not have made the enormous strides which led to the Belfast Agreement in April 1998 and the Referendum vote to support it six weeks later. The prisoners' involvement in the process once again highlights the political nature of their motivation, both as activists in the conflict and advocates of peace. In April 1995, when this matter was discussed in Dublin by the Forum for Peace and Reconciliation, Fianna Fáil TD Brian Lenihan's comments were pertinent:

> The nature of the conflict is political, the causes of the paramilitary organisations is political, the nature of the crime is political, the status of the prisoners is political, regardless of any official designation on the part of the British authorities.

This has been fully recognised and accepted by the signatories of the Belfast Agreement, albeit grudgingly by pro-agreement unionist politicians, and is clearly reflected in the provision made for early prisoner releases. When the agreement was signed there were around 400 paramilitary prisoners in Northern Ireland's prisons; at the time of writing there are around 200. It has even been mooted that by the end of the year 2000 the notorious Long Kesh H-Blocks themselves will have been expediently obliterated without trace.

A leading loyalist once told me that Billy McKee, PIRA commanding officer in Crumlin Road prison in 1970, had predicted that 'the war would end in the prisons'. In many ways McKee was right – in the long run the war did end in the prisons, but perhaps twenty years later than might otherwise have been the case.

Select Bibliography

Barrit, D.P. and C.F. Carter. *The Northern Ireland Problem: A Study in Community Relations*, Oxford University Press, Oxford, 1962

Bew, Paul and Gordon Gillespie. *Northern Ireland. A Chronology of the Troubles*, Gill and Macmillan, Dublin, 1993

Bew, Paul and Henry Patterson. *The British State and the Ulster Crisis*, Ben Paterson, London, 1985

Bonger, Willem A. *Criminality and Economic Conditions*, Little Brown, Boston, 1916

Bottomley, Keith. *Criminology in Focus*, M. Robertson and Co., Oxford, 1979

Boulding, K.E. *Conflict and Defence, General Theory*, Harper and Law, New York, 1963

Boulton, D. *The UVF 1966–73: An Anatomy of a Loyalist Rebellion*, Torc Books, Dublin, 1973

Bowyer Bell, J. *The Secret Army: A History of the IRA*, Academy Press, Dublin, 1979
The Irish Troubles: A Generation of Violence 1967–1992, Gill and Macmillan, Dublin, 1994

Bruce, Steve. *The Red Hand: Protestant Paramilitaries and the Northern Ireland Conflict*, Oxford University Press, Oxford, 1992

Crawford, Colin. 'Long Kesh: an alternative perspective', (unpublished M.Sc. thesis), Cranfield Institute of Technology, Bedford, 1980
'In defence of status: prison strategies and the Northern Ireland conflict' (unpublished M.Phil. thesis), University of Bradford, Bradford, 1993
Forbidden Femininity: Child Sexual Abuse and Female Sexuality, Ashgate Press, Aldershot, 1998

Cusack, J. and H. McDonald. *UVF: For God and Ulster*, Poolbeg, Dublin, 1997

Darby, John. *Conflict in Northern Ireland: The Development of a Polarised Community*, Gill and Macmillan, Dublin, 1976

Denzin, N.K. 'Collective behaviour in total institutions: the case of the mental hospital and prison', *Sociological Problems*, 15 (3), 1968

Durkheim, Émile. *Division of Labour in Society*, Free Press of Glencoe, New York, 1964

Ellis, Havelock. *The Criminal*, 3rd ed., Walter Scott, London, 1901

Ellis, M. 'The experience of Borstal', *New Society*, 11 October 1973

Ferri, Enrico. *The Positive School of Criminology*, C.H. Kerr, Chicago, 1913

Forum for Peace and Reconciliation, *Report of Proceedings*, vol. 13, 7 April 1995, Brunswick Press, Dublin, 1995

Fox, V. 'Prison disciplinary problems', in J. Johnston et al. (eds.), *Society of Punishment and Corrections*, Wiley and Sons, New York, 1962

Glasier, D. *The Effectiveness of a Prison and Parole System*, Bobbs, Merril, Indianapolis, 1964

Goffman, E. *Asylums*, Anchor Books, New York, 1961

Goffman, E. and J. Garfinkely. 'Conditions of successful degradation ceremonies', *American Journal of Sociology*, 61 (5), 1956

Hillyard, P. 'Law and order', in John Darby (ed.), *Northern Ireland: A Background to the Conflict*, Appletree Press/Syracuse University Press, Belfast and Syracuse, 1983

Jung, Carl G. *Four Archetypes*, Routledge and Kegan Paul, London, 1972

Kee, Robert. *Ireland, A History*, Abacus, London, 1982

Krista, A. *Deadlier than the Male: Violence and Aggression in Women*, Harper Collins, London, 1994

Lombroso, Cesare. *Crime, its Causes and Remedies*, Little Brown, Boston, 1918

McCorkle, Lloyd. 'Guard inmate relationships', in J. Johnston et al. (eds.), *Society of Punishment and Corrections*, Wiley and Sons, New York, 1962

Morrison, J. *The Ulster Cover Up*, Ulster Society, Armagh, 1983

Nelson, S. 'The Ulster independance debate', *Fortnight*, 14 January 1977

Northern Ireland Office White Paper, Cmnd 5675, HMSO, Belfast, 1975

O'Malley, Padraig. *The Uncivil Wars: Ireland Today*, Blackstaff Press, Belfast, 1983

Poole, M. 'The demography of violence', in John Darby (ed.), *Northern Ireland: A Background to the Conflict*, Appletree Press/Syracuse University Press, Belfast and Syracuse, 1983

Rolston, Bill. 'Reformism and sectarianism: state of the Union after civil rights', in John Darby (ed.), *Northern Ireland: A Background to the Conflict*, Appletree Press/Syracuse University Press, Belfast and Syracuse, 1983

Sabini, John. 'Aggression in the laboratory', in J.L. Kutash et al. (eds.), *Violence*, Josey Bass Inc., San Francisco, 1978

Schrag, Clarence. 'Leadership among prison inmates', in J. Johnston et al. (eds.), *Society of Punishment and Corrections*, Wiley and Sons, New York, 1962

Shimar, B. and A. Drory. *Criminal Justice and Behavior*, American Association of Correctional Psychologists, 8 (22), 1981

Sobel, Lester. *Political Prisoners, A World Report*, Facts on File Inc., New York, 1978

Sutherland, Edwin. *The Professional Thief*, University of Chicago Press, Chicago, 1937

Sykes, G.M. and M. Messenger. *The Inmate Social System: Theoretical Studies in the Social Organisation of the Prison*, Social Science Research Council, New York, 1960

White, J., J. Duffy and Colin Crawford. *Loyalist Political Prisoners in Context*,
   Post Conflict Resettlement Group, Belfast, 1997
Workers' Research Unit. *Belfast Bulletin*, no. 10, 1982
Zimbardo, Philip. 'The mind is a formidable jailer, A Pirandellian prison',
   New York Times Magazine, 8 April 1973

Index